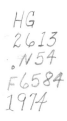

Citibank, Nader and the Facts

By Citibank

First National City Bank
399 Park Avenue, New York 10022

Citibank, Nader and the Facts: A Reply to
Ralph Nader's Study Group Report on First
National City Bank entitled "Citibank".
(Grossman Publishers, New York, 1973)

Library of Congress Catalogue Card Number 74-76559

Printed in the United States of America

Contents

PREFACE 1

I — Citibank Replies

A Statement by Walter B. Wriston, chairman 3

II — Chapter-by-Chapter Response

Introduction 17

1. Citibankers 18
2. Retail Banking for Individuals 22
3. Wholesale Banking for Corporations 28
4. Banking for Government 35
5. In Citibank We Trust 41
6. Bank Regulation 45
   Nader Appendices 49

III — Appendices to Citibank,
Nader and the Facts

1. Mr. Wriston's memos to Citibank staff 52
2. Published Data by the Investment 61
   Management Group

IV — Index 84

Preface

If the speed of modern communications, in a fashionable cliche, brings the peoples of the world closer together, it also keeps many of us further apart. Certainly, it separates the indictment ever further from the defense. This has surely been Citibank's experience with a book authored by one of Ralph Nader's study groups.

In a recent appearance before the United Nations inquiry on multinational corporations, Mr. Nader was challenged by one of the U.N. panel members for his reckless handling of facts and his extravagant rhetoric. Mr. Nader's ready response was that he was making "figurative use of language" to emphasize his conclusions. In claiming this indulgence, Mr. Nader appears to be asserting the right to take poetic license with the evidence in pursuit of a higher truth. Whatever one may think of Mr. Nader's methodology, it is certainly not the methodology of scholarship.

"Citibank," the book by David Leinsdorf and Donald Etra, is a sustained march from prejudicial assumptions to predetermined conclusions. Though it abounds in footnotes, the book's choice of facts and quotations is guided throughout by the determination to "make a case" against First National City Bank. The authors have not expended the smallest effort in trying to reach a balanced judgment on the bank's strengths and weaknesses.

As reflected in the accompanying reply, our dominant feeling is that we were ill-used. But we also acknowledge our keen disappointment. We originally entered into an agreement to talk with the Nader study group because we hoped that we might learn something about ourselves from a critical outside appraisal. We anticipated that the criticisms would be searching but that they would also be fair. We were wrong in our assumption. The study group was provided masses of information, but the authors of the report selected only those pieces which fit the indictment they were preparing. Information and unsubstantiated

1

charges obtained from other, usually anonymous sources were never cross-checked with us for accuracy or reply. Accordingly, despite the paraphernalia of scholarship with which the book is clothed, in our opinion it is a shoddy piece of merchandise. If anyone else had produced it, Ralph Nader would be demanding that it be recalled for repair.

Hence this short book. It is our attempt to catch up with the distortions of Nader's *Citibank*. Here you will find our general reply to that book together with point-by-point rebuttal of major issues. Finally, in the appendices we have included Mr. Walter Wriston's memos to the staff since there seems to be a question about what he did and did not say, and pertinent parts of our Investment Management Group's annual report for 1973.

Donald J. Colen
Vice President
Public Affairs

I — Citibank Replies

A general comment by Walter B. Wriston,
chairman of the First National City Bank,
on "Citibank", the book by Ralph Nader's
study group.

Ralph Nader's book on First National City Bank is basically a retread of his 1971 report. It reveals the same cynicism about other people's ethics and the same reckless misuse of facts and unsupported allegations to reach predetermined conclusions.

By basing a presumably scholarly study on the assumption that most, if not all, business relationships are essentially conspiratorial in nature, Mr. Nader and his associates forfeit the credibility that some of their earlier reports have justifiably earned.

Much of the information in the book is completely out of date. The only new chapter is one dealing with Citibank's trust operations, and this is riddled with errors of fact and interpretation.

The description of the Investment Management Group's (IMG's) activities also contains the same kind of contradictions that marked the 1971 study. We said then that 'it is difficult to know how to respond to a 550-page report which is on both sides of many issues.' It is still difficult.

On one page we are accused of allowing investments to lie dormant in trust accounts, on another of churning investments to produce activity. On one page an attempt to avoid capital gains is supposed to dictate our investment policies and on another our policies are alleged to incur unnecessary capital gains and liabilities for our customers.

But what disturbs us most about this book is the study group's irresponsible and multiplied use of the 'presumption of guilt' technique whereby it states its own unsubstantiated suspicions of alleged Citibank wrongdoing and then calls on us to prove otherwise. This is like asking a man to prove that he has never kicked his dog.

This approach is epitomized in the following statement on page 211 in the new section on our trust operations: "The principal ways a bank trust department can utilize trust funds for its own benefit are (a) to engage in 'broker reciprocity'; (b) to maintain large uninvested cash balances; (c) invest trust funds to support companies with commercial ties to the bank; and (d) to use trust funds to invest in its own stock."

The book's allegation that Citibank engages in these practices is false and based on completely unsubstantiated suppositions by the study group, as is pointed out in detail elsewhere in this reply.

Another glaring example of this technique is found on page 134 where the book comments on Citibank's processing of New York City income tax returns and the possibility of our misusing the information stored on computer tapes.

The report concedes that "city officials say FNCB has been doing an excellent job," concedes that "city officials monitor the bank's activities," and concedes that "the contract between FNCB and the city prohibits the bank from using the information extracted from the returns for other purposes."

Yet, without adducing a shred of evidence to support its contention, the report asserts that one reason Citibank got into the project "may have been the opportunity to use the information from the income tax returns in its credit files."

Still another use of this irresponsible "presumption of guilt" technique is found in the Nader "surrebuttal" to Citibank's response to the 1971 report. In denying that Citibank used commissions generated by New York City pension fund transactions to buy deposits for the bank from the brokerage house of Halsey Stuart & Co., I am correctly quoted as saying: "Not a single one of the Citibank-initiated orders was placed with Halsey Stuart.*" The asterisk refers to the following footnote: "At a press conference in June, 1971, the Nader Task Force conceded that the naming of Halsey Stuart could be wrong, but noted that Citibank has not produced evidence that the bank does not engage in reciprocity."

Using this same technique, the book makes allegations about dealings of other banks in Penn Central securities without acknowledging evidence in the public record that

(a) IMG's equity holdings in Penn Central were negligible and its bond and related security holdings were comparatively small and (b) IMG did not foresee developments in time to dispose of these holdings even though Citibank's commercial loan department was fully aware of Penn Central's worsening financial situation.

Acknowledgement of these well-known facts would clearly have weakened the study group's charge that there is an exchange of information between the trust department and the commercial side of the bank.

The Nader group will no doubt respond by complaining, as it has so often done, about our alleged "failure to cooperate." After publication of the first study group report, we did, indeed, decline to spend additional time with Mr. Nader's associates in further discussions of IMG's activities.

But we did so because the first report largely ignored the vast store of information provided to the study group through interviews that lasted hundreds of hours and cost the bank many thousands of dollars.

The first report was based in large part on information developed from outside sources, much of it erroneous. We were not given the courtesy of being asked to comment on this information. Under the circumstances, we simply could not justify more such unproductive use of bank time or wasteful expense to our stockholders.

The book repeatedly attacks Citibank for failure to make public disclosure. This charge is baseless. The amount of information which Citibank supplies annually to state and federal authorities is immense, and our records are, by law, open to the various regulatory agencies. Four years ago, ours was the first bank trust department to publish an accounting of our investments, purchases and sales, performance and policies, an innovative step nowhere acknowledged by the study group.

The problem is that Mr. Nader and his associates claim the right to represent the public and to receive data which the U.S. Congress and the New York State Legislature have authorized various public agencies to receive. The study group treats disclosure to the duly constituted authorities as if it were a form of concealment. The quarrel which the study group has in this instance, as in many others, is with federal and state laws and regulatory authorities, not with us.

For our part, we do not believe we have any obligation to give Mr. Nader's associates information about confidential relationships between Citibank and its customers, to reveal data which we consider to be of value to our competitors or to provide them with any other facts, documents or opinions not generally available to the public. The study group was determined to hang us, despite no evidence of guilt. Having once experienced the sensation of a kangaroo court, the hangee simply did not feel obliged in this case to cooperate the second time around.

Citibank is not immune to errors in judgment and in practice, but we never stop trying to correct them. That's why we regularly have outside consultants audit our performance and recommend ways to improve it. However, the Nader group perversely utilizes these consultant studies to belabor the very practices which have been changed or eliminated as a result of those studies.

In the past three years, for example, we have greatly improved our personal loan collection procedures and made scores of other improvements ranging from the elimination of noise in work areas to simplification in loan forms.

The study group has ignored this progress while unfairly resorting to selective updating in the original study to support its own rigid preconceptions.

While we categorically reject the central thesis of this report, we will, nevertheless, examine individual criticism on its merits and where the charges are valid, make appropriate changes in policy or practice.

It is obviously impossible to respond here to all of the charges and issues raised in a book-length manuscript. We do, however, feel we must answer other major inaccuracies in the book with the following facts:

Voting Citicorp Stock: The study group makes the accusation that Citibank uses trust funds to its own advantage by investing in Citicorp stock and voting that stock to perpetuate management control of the corporation.

The facts are that the IMG never buys Citicorp stock except when it is instructed to do so by employees participating in the bank's profit sharing plan, or when it is specifically instructed to do so by a customer. The IMG never votes Citicorp stock under any circumstances. These facts could readily have been ascertained by the study group from reports published annually by the IMG.

As a matter of policy, the IMG never expresses an opinion on Citicorp stock even in cases where IMG customers insist on having it in their portfolios. Citicorp stock is carried in a customer's portfolio only upon receipt of his written instructions to that effect.

Relations between Investment Department and Commercial Side — "The Wall": The book is replete with unfortunate, totally unwarranted implications regarding relations between the Investment Management Group and other departments of the bank. It implies, for example, that IMG has access to credit files of the lending departments, which is flatly prohibited by the bank's policy manual. Within IMG, the investment function is under total control of our Investment Policy Committee presided over by Senior Vice President Paul Collins, who is specifically prohibited from querying commercial files. No senior officers of the bank, including the head of the IMG, sit on that committee. Citibank senior management learns of individual buy-and-sell decisions only after such action has been taken.

The book refers to an Investment Policy Committee (page 164) and an Investment Policy Board (page 248) composed of senior Citicorp officials. That Investment Policy Committee, on which Messrs. Wriston, Spencer, Palmer,

Laeri and Wilcox sat, was disbanded in January, 1971, before the original Nader report was completed.

At one time, these same officers sat on both the Board of Directors of the bank and the Trust Board of the bank. The Trust Board was dissolved nearly two years ago. Mr. Wilcox resigned from the bank over two years ago. Mr. Laeri retired in April, 1971.

IMG's Investment Performance: In examining the performance of the Investment Management Group's common trust funds for personal trusts and for pension funds, the study group utilized a time period when the stock market generally was declining. Having selected such a time frame, the authors then emphasize that certain Citibank funds lost ground during that period. We think it is significant, however, that the study group's own figures show that the comparable market indices were outperformed by three of Citibank's four common trust funds for personal accounts (page 190) and by eight of the nine funds for pension accounts (page 214). In three cases, the difference in performance was more than 20 percentage points and in four cases more than 10 percentage points.

Neither Citibank nor any other reliable investment adviser claims that the investments it recommends will always increase in value, regardless of market trends. The only sensible basis for evaluating investment performance is on a comparative basis. And properly interpreted, the study group's own figures prove that Citibank's performance was considerably better than average.

Investment in Director-Affiliated Companies: Relationships between Citicorp and a particular corporation have no effect on IMG's investment decisions. There have been instances where IMG has completely sold off discretionary holdings in a corporation's stock despite director affiliations in both directions, when the Investment Research Department concluded that the interests of IMG customers would be served by selling.

9

The annual reports of IMG show that in 1971 and 1972, for example, IMG made substantial sales of securities of several corporations with which Citicorp has director-affiliations, e.g., NCR, Monsanto, Exxon, Sears and Xerox. During this period, IMG also purchased stock in companies with director affiliations and in certain cases, IBM and ITT, for example, both bought and sold large blocks of stock. These buy-and-sell decisions were made without any flow of information from the director level or from the commercial side and without regard to the particular interests of the affected corporation.

IMG's sole responsibility is to the investment customers it serves. We know of no case in which Citicorp or Citibank management or directors have asked IMG to buy or to refrain from selling securities in order to help a particular company or have provided IMG with information on a company's prospects.

In the highly competitive investment management business, Citibank could not long survive if non-investment considerations had any influence on purchase and sale decisions.

Uninvested Cash Balances: The study group suggests, incorrectly, that the Investment Management Group deliberately keeps a portion of its customers' holdings in cash so that the bank may profit from use of the uninvested balances. In the case of trust accounts under our management, cash balances represent less than 7/10 of 1% of total assets under management. Half of this amount is simply income accumulated between disbursements to beneficiaries and the rest is temporary cash balances arising between purchases and sales of securities. In the case of custodial accounts, any uncommitted balances are under the customer's direction. In all cases, the amount of cash in an account is reported regularly in each customer, is subject to regulatory review and is reported in the aggregate in the IMG's widely distributed annual report.

Broker Reciprocity: The study group makes much of the issue of "broker reciprocity"; i.e., commission transactions based on broker deposits. Although the report quotes our denials, it implies nevertheless that the practice does exist. We think it is useful to state the facts unequivocally.

Our corporate policy manual, in a statement dated November 10, 1970, makes it clear that selection of brokers and dealers to execute equity security transactions for Citibank customers is the sole province of the Investment Management Group.

The policy statement clearly says that "in selecting brokers, no recognition will be given to the fact that a broker maintains deposit balances with the bank or transacts other business with the Investment Management Group or other departments or branches of the bank."

The Comptroller's Department in the bank audits broker selections twice a year to assure that proper procedures are followed. IMG's primary consideration in selecting a broker for a particular transaction is whether "the best available execution is obtained on all trades for the accounts of customers." Senior Vice President Paul Collins and the head security trader are the only persons in Citibank who know what each broker receives in commissions at the time the allocations are made, and they are specifically barred from receiving information about any broker's relationships with the commercial side of the bank.

Favoritism to Corporate Customers: The study group accuses Citibank of favoring corporate customers over individual borrowers, although it concedes that Citibank makes many more personal loans than any other New York bank. While acknowledging Citibank's large volume of installment loans, the study group nevertheless contends that funds are disproportionately allocated to big borrowers.

For example, the bank is accused of having made loans to support the acquisition of Harvey Aluminum, Amerada Petroleum and Sinclair Oil in 1969 after the Federal Reserve

11

Board had switched to a restrictive monetary policy. The facts are that the Hess-Amerada merger took place through an exchange of shares without bank financing and that the credit extensions in the other two cases were made in 1968, although the mergers were not consummated until 1969.

The book likewise asserts that during the 1970-71 recession, the lending rate to major corporate customers declined to 5.25% from a 1970 peak of 8.5%, while personal lending rates were reduced approximately 0.5%. The study group does not seem to consider it worth mentioning that the base lending rate for major corporate customers is now at $9\frac{3}{4}$%, while personal installment lending rates are at approximately the 1968 level.

Research Methodology: Much is made of a so-called "random sampling" of Citibank trust accounts, based on 25 replies to the study group's questionnaire. Interestingly, four out of five of the people contacted by the study group declined to answer their questionnaires. But more fundamentally, Citibank has 10,000 such accounts, some large, some small, with obviously differing investment objectives. Under these conditions, as any reliable opinion analyst will attest, a totally random sample is meaningless and only a "stratified sample" has validity. Moreover, according to the experts, a survey of 25 accounts in order to gain a representation of 10,000 accounts could lead to statistical errors as high as 80%.

Alleged Nondisclosure of Interest Charges: Citibank is accused of failing to disclose interest rate charges on its Checking Plus accounts, failing to explain the repayment procedure on Checking Plus overdrafts and of neglecting to mention overdraft charges on personal checking accounts. Wrong again. A brochure mailed to all approved applicants of Checking Plus clearly states how the finance charge is determined and applied and also states the resulting annual percentage rate.

As to the method of repayment, the brochure says:

"Checking Plus loan payments and checking account deposits are handled separately: deposits made to your checking account will not be applied to pay or prepay your Checking Plus loan balance. Payments must be made either by mail . . . or in person at any branch, accompanied by the payment ticket section of the Statement or a proper notice of prepayment." Any paying or receiving teller will accept such payments. The study group is incorrect in stating that the customer must go to a special window.

With regard to overdraft charges, a list of "Rules Governing First Class Checking Accounts" sent to all new customers states: "The account may be charged $2.50 in respect of each stop-payment order (and) $4 in respect of return of an item drawn against unavailable or insufficient funds."

The Master Charge form reproduced in the book (page 37) has not been in use since September, 1971. The present form emphasizes the amount which must be paid to avoid finance charges. This is another instance where the study group preferred to ignore readily available current information in order to "substantiate" its outdated accusations.

Personnel Practices: The chapter on Citibankers is one of several instances where information to indict Citibank for "not caring" is derived from several studies, some of which Citibank itself commissioned precisely in order to identify and correct deficiencies.

In regard to employees salaries, the book deduces from a U.S. Department of Labor funded study by Professor R. David Corwin of New York University that in FNCB salary grades six through nine, "approximately 90 percent of the employees make $6,500 or less." The Nader study group goes on to argue that it is reasonable to conclude that the vast majority of Citibank's clerical workers earn less than $6,500" and that according to the U.S. Department of Labor, it took $7,183 in early 1970 for a New York City family of four to sustain a low standard of living.

First, FNCB salary grades six through nine represent less than half of Citibank's total work force and those employees are by and large in entry level positions. Second, at the time of the study, the average clerical salary was in excess of the U.S. Department of Labor's $7,183 figure.

By definition, most of our entry level employees are young and inexperienced. As the Bureau of Labor Statistics points out regarding the $7,183 figure used by the study group, it "should be compared directly only with the total annual income of urban four-person, husband-wife families, a nonworking wife and a husband 35-44 years old who works full time."

Citibank employees do not remain at their entry level salaries. During the period discussed in the Nader report, Citibank's 15,900 non-official employees in New York received 16,512 merit salary increases and 7,400 promotion increases. The report is simply incorrect.

Shortly after publication of the preliminary Nader study group report in 1971, Professor Corwin issued the following statement: "In seeking to point out what are deficiencies in personnel practices and policies especially as they relate to minorities, the Nader report fails to take cognizance of several important facts. In recent years, banks in New York City have been in the vanguard of equal employment opportunity hiring for clerical personnel. Although they have been pushed in this direction by labor market conditions they have also been pulled by key executive officers. Of the banks in New York, First National City Bank has been one of the most progressive institutions. While racial problems remain, Citibank is in several important aspects ahead of other banking institutions in their thinking and actions. This is especially true with regard to promotional opportunities for clerical employees. The banking industry in general and Citibank in particular have developed a variety of successful affirmative action programs that fail to come to light in the

Nader report. In this sense it is incomplete."

The Nader report's allegations regarding minority employment are also off-target. Our record of increasing minority representation as a percentage of total staff has been much better than that of the banking industry as a whole, which has posted the largest gains of any U.S. industry. "No other industry runs even a 'close second,'" according to David A. Sawyer, director of the Treasury Department's Equal Opportunity Program. Minority representation in management-level positions at Citibank has also been increasing and minority recruitment has been assigned top priority in Citibank's college recruitment program.

Allegations regarding the role of women at Citibank offer an example of selective updating. Citibank currently has nine women vice presidents, not one as the study asserts, and 35 women assistant vice presidents as well. The study group did not update this information, although it reported about a one-day picketing of Citibank corporate headquarters by the National Organization of Women, a development which occurred after publication of the first report.

II — Chapter-by-Chapter Response

Point-by-point, errors and accusations
made by the Nader Group are rebutted
in this section.

Comment on the Foreword by Ralph Nader

Mr. Nader's foreword is a distillation of the most extreme charges contained in the report. His description of Citibank bears little relation to the real world of banking at Citibank or at other financial institutions. Our answers to his charges are in our general reply and at the appropriate place in this chapter-by-chapter response.

Introduction

The first part of the Introduction is largely a summary of the principal charges and recommendations against the bank. It later becomes a complaint about Citibank's failure to provide the study group with information which it demanded. There are three points we wish to make on this score:

1. Much of the information we are accused of failing to disclose is freely available in our annual report. Our 1972 report, for example, contains a listing of Citicorp subsidiaries and a brief description of their activities, figures on total loan commitments, both domestic and foreign, the size of our loan commitments to other financial institutions, etc.

2. From the outset we made it crystal clear to Mr. Nader's associates that a bank's relationships with its customers are, by their very nature, highly private and personal, and that Citibank would not disclose such confidential information nor any information which would be of value to Citibank's competitors.

Most if not all of the information Mr. Nader's associates criticized us for withholding falls into one or the other category. We are astounded, for example, that the Nader task force could regard "the names of companies whose loans had been written off as losses" as anything other than confidential. Similarly, it is difficult to understand how they could view loans to individual industries or a breakdown of checking or time deposits by size as information of no value to our competitors.

3. Here, and indeed throughout the book, the Nader study group makes the unspoken assumption that information denied to them is information totally denied to an interested public. This is not the case.

Citibank regularly submits massive quantities of data to federal and state regulatory agencies, as duly provided by law. In addition, its books are automatically opened to federal and state bank examiners, and needed data are available to other public officials with proper legal authorization.

Although they have tried to assume the role, the Nader study group has not been either elected or appointed to represent the public interest. Certainly we cannot abdicate judgment on what is confidential or competitive information to Mr. Nader's associates.

I-Citibankers

This section is based to a substantial extent on an outside consultant study, which Citibank itself commissioned as a guide to improvement of its personnel practices, and a U.S. Department of Labor funded study on hiring practice of New York City banks by Professor R. David Corwin of New York University. Obviously we would not have gone to the considerable expense of commissioning a study if we were entirely satisfied with existing policies and intended to make no changes. Even so, the Nader report inaccurately reflects the substance of the studies themselves.

As might be expected, the reports contained a number of comparisons and comments, some of them critical, some complimentary. The Nader study group typically discarded anything that might be considered to reflect favorably on First National City Bank.

In citing the study of bank hiring practices conducted by Professor Corwin (page 2), the Nader study group conveys the impression that Professor Corwin was harshly critical of Citibank. Quite the contrary, Professor Corwin, in a press release issued in 1971 to correct this impression, refers to Citibank as the best employer among New York City banks.

In this section, as elsewhere in the report, the study group jumps from a small nugget of information to wildly inaccurate conclusions. Our response to Nader's statement that in FNCB salary grades 6-9, "approximately 90 percent of the employees make $6,500 or less" is found in the statement by Mr. Wriston. (Personnel Practices — page 13.)

The report's comments regarding Citibank participation in the JOBS program are unfair and inaccurate. This is a program aimed at training and hiring the hard-core unemployed or under-employed. Over and above reimbursement received from the Department of Labor, the JOBS program costs Citibank nearly three times normal hiring and training costs per employee. In spite of this, Citibank at the time was the nation's largest single participant in the training of office clerical employees under this program.

The Nader report acknowledges (page 4) that Citibank's JOBS program "has brought people with no job skills and non-existent or spotty employment histories into the labor force" but then goes on to fault us for failing to upgrade entry level employees.

Aside from the fact that this is mixing apples and oranges, it also happens to be inaccurate. Citibank has an active program for helping employees improve their skills through on-the-job training and to advance educationally by means of our high school equivalency, English as a second language and tuition refund programs.

The report's allegations regarding minority employment at Citibank (page 5 ff) are also answered in the foregoing Citibank statement. (Personnel Practices — page 13.)

The report's description of the complaint against Citibank by Beverly Wadsworth (pages 10-11) is highly prejudicial. The charges which she made were dismissed by the

New York State Division of Human Rights on August 31, 1973, though the case is now on appeal. Undisputed evidence adduced during the hearing disclosed that Ms. Wadsworth was hired into the credit management training program of the bank's then Metropolitan Division on October 14, 1968. She was one of 24 new hires in the program that year. The other 23 hires were all male.

Of the 24 new hires in her program, she received the fourth highest starting salary; after 18 months, she was receiving the highest salary. Ms. Wadsworth was advanced faster than any other member of her training program and was recommended for officership 20 months after hire.

On July 23, 1970, a little more than 21 months after hire, she submitted a letter of resignation stating that she wished to continue her education at the Columbia Graduate School of Business Administration.

Under cross-examination, Ms. Wadsworth admitted that she could not point to any other member of her training program who had fared as well as she had fared at the bank. Instead, she then complained about the allegedly faster progress of a black male trainee who was in a different entry-level program that was not in existence until after she had been hired.

The section entitled "The Factory" ignores Citibank's efforts to improve working conditions, omits to say that the study it quotes was prepared for Citibank and suppresses any comments favorable to the bank.

The Opinion Research Corporation study that the book quotes from (page 14 ff) concluded:

> "A large majority of clerical staff members view the bank favorably as a place to work. This view has not changed much since the 1966 survey, indicating that Citibank has done a reasonably good job of maintaining basic staff morale. This is especially encouraging in light of the fact that in recent years the levels of favorable response on questions like this (regarding other institutions) have generally declined."

The Nader report wrongly asserts that "all Operating Group clericals" responded to the ORC survey. In fact, only 29 percent returned their questionnaires. As any student of opinion research knows, self-selected samples do not necessarily furnish a reliable guide to attitudes of a larger population.

This technique can be useful, however, in spotlighting potential problems for additional analysis. The Nader quotations, indeed, are drawn, not from the full ORC study, but from an internal analysis of the survey's negative features. This analysis was made precisely to indicate where more detailed investigation was required to verify or amplify the results obtained in the initial survey.

As a result, we took a number of steps to remedy employee complaints. These included carpeting a floor containing heavy machinery and introducing earplugs custom-fitted by Citibank's medical department to reduce the noise level; using a taste panel and a rating card system to improve cafeteria food; instituting 24-hour a day medical service; creating a new information program to keep employees abreast of changes affecting them; modernizing and redecorating work areas; and establishing a new training program for all supervisors designed to give them a better understanding of the bank's personnel policies, and to equip them to help employees advance and to improve their on-the-job performance.

We long have had a successful suggestion award program and a problem review procedure whereby employees' problems are promptly and fairly reviewed and resolved. We recently established a service called "Citiline" which enables employees to communicate comments or complaints to management on a strictly confidential basis with assurance of a prompt response. Obviously, there are always problems and there is always room for improvement. But we think Citibank has demonstrated that it is actively concerned with the views of its employees.

II — Retail Banking for Individuals

Like the preceding chapter, this part begins with extensive quotations from reports which First National City Bank commissioned in order to monitor and improve retail customer service. Again, by failing to ask us about these reports during their numerous conversations with bank personnel, the Nader study group saved itself the trouble of taking into account the extensive changes which have been made to improve our services as a result of the consultant's study.

Service: To remedy platform service problems discussed in the Cresap, McCormick and Paget study entitled "Third Service Shopping Program," Citibank instituted specialized courses in Product Knowledge and Basic Interviewing, as well as related courses such as Advanced Consumer Credit, Secured Lending and others.

Since these courses began, more than 1,000 platform people have attended the Product Knowledge course and an equal number the Basic Interviewing course. Another 1,000 people have had one or more of the additional courses.

Self-teaching courses and special presentations are also made available on a number of subjects. Simplified application forms and other documents have been developed to reduce interview time, and we are now in some branches using service counters in place of desks on branch platforms. These steps have materially reduced the service problems outlined in the Cresap study.

Checking Accounts: The report makes various inaccurate statements regarding Citibank checking account services which are answered in Citibank's statement. (Alleged Nondisclosure of Interest Charges — page 12.)

Personal Loans: The heart of this section is its attack on Citibank's credit extension and collection practices. The

22

report alleges that Citibank, in its eagerness "to develop a customer relationship that may turn profitable in the future," deliberately makes loans "to thousands of people who simply cannot afford to pay." The allegation is utterly false.

Citibank makes more loans to lower-income individuals than the next several major New York City banks combined, and it is proud of this fact. But contrary to the Nader thesis, credit overloading is an infrequent cause of default.

The very work on which Mr. Nader's associates lean so heavily, Columbia University Professor David Caplovitz' "Debtors in Default," finds that defaulting debtors themselves mention "voluntary over-extension" of credit as the primary cause of default in only 13 percent of the cases.

Professor Caplovitz also has a category labeled "involuntary over-extension" cited as accounting for another five percent of the defaults, but the text reveals that the category would more accurately have been described as unexpected demands on income.

In any case, Citibank's lending standards, embodied in instructions which our personal lending officers are required to follow, are quite explicit about the obligation to avoid overloading the borrower.

The Nader report asserts, however, that "about 30 percent of its defaulting debtors . . . obtain credit in violation of Citibank's own debt-to-income guidelines." This statistic is derived from research done by Professor Caplovitz for his informative and scholarly study, but it is quite recklessly applied.

Professor Caplovitz is careful to acknowledge that his study "is based entirely on interviews with debtors in default. At no point did we interview . . . their creditors." The Nader report, of course, makes no mention of this essential qualification. It simply takes the allegation as the fact.

Among debtors interviewed for Professor Caplovitz' study were a total of 35 out of 500,000 Citibank borrowers, of whom a total of 11 asserted that they were over the

23

debt-to-income limit. Indeed, based on the Nader version of the interviews taken from Professor Caplovitz' files, several of the 11 did not allege that their obligations to Citibank exceeded the debt-to-income guideline — only that their obligations to Citibank plus other pre-existing obligations put them over the limit.

The size of the sample from which these sweeping statistical conclusions are extrapolated, the unquestioning acceptance of statements obtained from debtors anxious to justify their position and the failure even to consider the possibility that some pre-existing obligations may have been deliberately concealed from Citibank loan officers suggest the mushy foundation on which the report's judgments rest.

Suffice it to say that Citibank's own information completely contradicts the contention that there has been a substantial breakdown in application of the debt-to-income guideline. Indeed, Citibank's delinquency record in recent years has been better than the average of other New York State and New York City banks.

The Nader report acknowledges (page 32) that "it is important for poor people to obtain credit at banks, because their rates are lower than those of the small loan companies."

But it complains that Citibank's collection policies are unfairly weighted against lower income persons. Thus, the report contends that persons with incomes of $5,000 or less constitute more than 50 percent of Citibank debtors in default (page 64).

How these figures were arrived at is not clearly explained, but presumably they involve the same 35 Citibank borrowers interviewed for the Caplovitz study. At least that is the source cited. To check the facts, Citibank itself made an analysis of 550 loans called or "matured" in a typical month. Of that number, 27.8 percent had incomes of less than $6,000, 27.3 percent had incomes of $6,000 to $7,500, 21.6 percent had incomes of $7,500 to $10,000, 13.5 per-

24

cent were in the $10,000 to $15,000 category and 4.4 percent exceeded $15,000.

Citibank's analysis reveals a higher proportion of delinquencies among lower income borrowers, as might be expected, but the real figures are nowhere near those put forward in the Nader book. Possibly the Nader investigators are talking about the earnings at the time the debtor defaulted. Since loss of income is by far the most important reason for debtor default, that is at least a plausible explanation. But if that is the basis for the Nader figures, they are not relevant to a discussion of Citibank lending practices. Citibank makes a judgment based on an applicant's past history and present earnings; it cannot see into the future.

Master Charge: The Nader report's statement (page 36) that Citibank's Master Charge billing statement "violates the Truth-in-Lending Act and Regulation Z" is another error. Our current forms, in use since September, 1971, give greater emphasis to the "new balance." We have a written opinion from the Office of the Comptroller of the Currency that the periodic billing statements of Master Charge, as well as all our other periodic billing statements for revolving credit, are in substantial compliance with Regulation Z.

Citibank's control procedures for Master Charge merchants initially emphasize the merchant's experience with other card issuers and includes a check with Better Business Bureau files and a visit to the merchant's premises. Complaint files are maintained on all merchants and those generating a disproportionate number of complaints are warned. If complaints persist without satisfactory explanation, the relationship is ended.

Collection Practices: As for its criticism of Citibank's collection practices, the Nader report again overstates the facts. "Adjusted for the volume of consumer credit outstanding," the report says, Citibank's "rate of suit is way out of proportion," (page 54). It is true that during the period covered by the Nader study, Citibank sued more frequently than other banks. But it also made nearly three times as many personal loans as its nearest competitor and almost as many total loans as its four major competitors combined.

Furthermore, Citibank's personal loan portfolio contained many more unsecured loans than its competitor's portfolios (70 percent of total loans as of December 31, 1969, compared to 58 percent for the four major competitors combined). Resort to the courts is the only remedy available to a creditor when a debtor defaults on an unsecured loan.

Moreover, Citibank has made a number of changes designed to improve communications between bank and borrower and to make it clear at all stages of the collection process that Citibank is willing to work matters out with a delinquent debtor whenever possible.

Before a summons is issued, our procedures now call for an attorney's letter again requesting payment and suggesting that the debtor make arrangements with the bank. All letters include a telephone number to call, and our collection department has been reorganized in an effort to keep the same collector on a particular account so as to make relations more personal.

These changes have substantially reduced customer complaints and have also reduced the percentage of cases which must be taken to court. Instructions regarding threatening telephone contacts, calls at unreasonable hours and conversations that might conceivably jeopardize a debtor's employment have been strengthened and surveillance has been increased.

Likewise, Citibank has taken further steps to try to assure effective service of summons when required. Our attorney now sends out a post-service letter notifying each debtor that we "have received an affidavit from a process server stating that you have been served" and inviting discussion of the case with the debtor or his attorney.

This method provides a 100 percent audit of service. In addition, we have been spot checking process servers by sending summonses to fictitious debtors. If these are reported as served, the company is notified that the offending process server is to do no further business on behalf of Citibank. Despite these steps, we believe that the "sewer service" problem cannot be completely eliminated without a change in New York State's archaic process-serving law.

Contrary to the impression conveyed by the report, we believe that Citibank's collection policies are currently among the least onerous and most conciliatory employed by any major consumer lender in the country. We continue, however, to expect to be repaid when we make a loan, and as long as debtors default, collection activities will continue to be necessary.

III — Wholesale Banking for Corporations

Who Gets Credit? Betraying its fundamental misunderstanding of the economic function performed by the banking system, the Nader report complains that Citibank makes fewer loans, relative to deposits, at branches serving primarily residential areas than at branches serving commercial or industrial customers. Of course that is the case.

Banks exist to attract excess funds and to lend those funds to persons, companies and governmental bodies in need of additional capital. Individual demand deposits and savings are a substantial source of supply, and business is a principal source of demand.

Thus the "loan-to-deposit ratios" decried by the report (page 82) are an inherent, indeed necessary, characteristic of a multibranch commercial bank. Citibank certainly recognizes a responsibility to the communities in which it operates, but engaging in distortion of the market mechanism is not an appropriate or effective way to help.

The study group's allegations regarding favoritism to corporate customers are answered in Mr. Wriston's statement. (Favoritism to Corporate Customers — page 11.)

Financing Corporate Concentration: The Hess Oil-Amerada Oil merger which Citibank is alleged to have financed came about through an exchange of shares. No bank financing was involved.

Citibank participated to the extent of $60 million in a $432.5 million revolving credit agreement with Atlantic Richfield to permit that company to counter a tender offer for Sinclair common stock by Gulf & Western. The loan agreement with Atlantic Richfield was concluded in 1968. The purchase of Sinclair stock was completed on December 23, 1968, although the merger itself did not become effective until March 4, 1969.

The Martin Marietta-Harvey Aluminum merger was accomplished through a public offering of subordinated debentures and an exchange of stock, use of corporate cash and some bank financing. Although the transaction was not completed until late 1969, it was initiated in 1968. Citibank's participation consisted of a $10.4 million share in an $80 million loan arrangement headed by Mellon Bank which was dated November 1, 1968.

Thus, the Nader report is wrong in asserting that the Amerada, Sinclair and Harvey acquisitions contradict Citibank's statement that it stopped making acquisition loans in 1969 in response to a Federal Reserve Board policy shift. There was no loan involved in the Hess-Amerada merger, and credit extensions in the other two cases took place in 1968, even though the mergers were not formally completed until 1969. The study group could easily have learned these facts if it had inquired during the first phase of the study.

"Equity Kickers": Citibank Vice Chairman George C. Scott, since retired as the bank's senior credit officer, wrote a memorandum on July 1, 1971 which stated: "We have decided that henceforth we shall not, as a matter of bank policy, take warrants, including so-called 'shadow' warrants," except under direct supervision of the Credit Policy Committee. Only one such transaction has been approved since that time. In short, Citibank prefers to avoid this practice, although there may be individual circumstances in which it is an appropriate way to compensate the bank for participation in a growth situation where the borrower cannot afford a more direct form of payment. Contrary to the unattributed assertion by "many former Citibank officers," equity kickers were never "common" at Citibank.

Flying High With No Money Down: The first thing that must be said about this section is that no one in the Corporate Banking Group was ever interviewed by Mr. Nader's associates regarding relations with aircraft manufacturers or the airline industry. Except for some peripheral facts elicited from a vice president of the bank's leasing subsidiary, all the information and mis-information came from other sources. Second, while this book purports to be about Citibank, much of the material in this section relates to others.

Citibank emphatically denies any suggestion that it put additional money into aircraft manufacturers to protect its original loans or that it lends money to airlines to create a market for the manufacturers. Each borrower is evaluated independently. We make our loans strictly on the basis of credit-worthiness and the economic justification presented for the loan.

We also deny that we equate credit-worthiness with size. The fact is that we have not made a commitment to finance an airline at the prime rate since August 1, 1968. Furthermore, contrary to the report, neither the credit agreement with McDonnell Douglas nor the one with Boeing was at the prime rate. The Lockheed agreement called for an increase on December 31, 1971, from the prime to one quarter of one percent over the prime.

This part concludes with a section on the financial problems of aircraft manufacturers, with particular emphasis on the federal government's decision to guarantee $250 million in additional loans to Lockheed. The implication is that banks originally lent money to Lockheed without taking adequate care and were bailed out by the U.S. government.

At the time Citibank made its loan decision in May, 1969, Lockheed had enjoyed eight consecutive profitable years. While there were preliminary indications of differences with the Defense Department over the C5A project, there was no evidence that these disagreements would result in catastrophic financial impairment of the company.

Furthermore, despite everything, Lockheed could have moved ahead with the L-1011 airbus except for the bankruptcy of Rolls Royce. As a condition of going ahead with the Rolls Royce engine, the British government insisted that the U.S. step in.

30

The U.S. weighed the economic consequences, including not only the potential failure of a prime defense contractor but also the resulting impact on Lockheed employees and plant locations, as well as the effect on subcontractors and on airlines which had made prepayments on the L-1011. The Nixon Administration decided to intervene, and the Congress concurred.

Potential losses to banks were a relatively minor consideration in these deliberations. As several banking witnesses testified during Congressional hearings, the banks could have withstood a Lockheed bankruptcy without critical difficulty.

The airline credit table in the Nader report is wrong with respect to almost every figure shown. The aircraft leasing figure employed in the report is also incorrect. As of June 30, 1972, the aggregate original investment of Citibank for its own account in the cost of aircraft under lease to all U.S. air carriers was approximately $192 million.

Aircraft leasing takes place under a ruling from the Internal Revenue Service approving such transactions. The equipment decisions themselves are made by the airlines. Depending on their own situation, some airlines prefer to buy their own planes, others prefer leasing and still others buy some planes and lease others.

The assertion that Citibank "shares directors" with a number of aircraft manufacturers and airlines is false. One Citibank official serves on the board of United Aircraft and an executive of United Aircraft serves on the Citicorp board. Walter Wriston is a director of General Electric, which manufactures aircraft engines but is not primarily an aerospace company. With these exceptions, there are no director affiliations between Citicorp and the aerospace industries.

First National City's Board of Directors: The report states (page 109) that Citibank in 1970 "was interlocked with 40 of the 300 largest industrial corporations in America, including seven of the top 10, six of the 15 largest life insurance companies, two of the four largest retailing companies and the two largest utilities.

The large number of affiliations cited by the report depends on the concept of third-party affiliations, which is totally illogical. These allegedly exist when John Doe, a member of the Citicorp board, also serves on the board of the ABC Company with Richard Roe, who is in turn a member of the DEF Company board.

Under the concept of the third-party affiliation, Citicorp and the DEF Company are said to be affiliated because Mr. Doe and Mr. Roe serve together on the ABC Company board. Thus, one of Mr. Nader's satellite groups has asserted that Citibank has affiliations with seven airlines although not one member of Citibank's board of directors serves on the board of any airline. All the alleged affiliations with airlines are of the third-party variety.

Who Doesn't Get Credit? — The discussion of Citibank's economic development activity reflects lack of up-to-date knowledge. Several years ago, Citicorp's urban affairs efforts were substantially revised and placed under the continuing surveillance of a top management committee and an advisory group of more junior employees. Citibank's volume of loans to minority business has been considerably increased, and more emphasis has been placed on follow-through and on consulting relationships with loan recipients. The revised program makes funds available to small as well as to big enterprises.

An Economic Development Center with a full-time professional staff has been set up to handle situations requiring specialized know-how or a centralized financial capability. This unit evaluates loan applications and works closely with clients on financial planning matters. As compared to previous arrangements which tended to be more passive, the Economic Development Center actively works to generate referrals for our combined loan and investment programs from the branch system and from other sources, most particularly community-based local development corporations.

Most community development activities, including more conventional business loans, continue to take place through the branches. However, specialized units have been set up to handle the complexities of lending for housing and community facilities, contributions to local groups and such human resources programs as jobs counseling and consumer education. In addition, in order to increase effectiveness of branch-level activities, Citibank now has community affairs officers working in Brooklyn, Staten Island, Queens, and the Bronx. Their job is to make Citibank's urban service facilities available to local organizations at the borough level, to analyze local market needs and to recommend new responses. We also have a street banker program operating in South Jamaica.

At present, in the lowest income areas served by Citibank, net deposits are substantially retained in the community through loans and other commitments for personal, business and construction financing.

Exceeding Lending Limits: This section (page 92 ff) is a compound of fact, fantasy and misinterpretation. The report alleges that loans are often made in violation of the bank's lending policies which normally require three officers to approve any sizable loan.

Individual account officers do make commitments to customers without obtaining the prior approval of their superiors, but they are expected to exercise good judgment based on their intimate knowledge of a particular account.

The requirement that loans be approved by two additional bank officers provides a backstop or review of the account officer's judgment. Occasionally, an account officer will make a loan commitment at too low a price. Basic credit errors almost never occur.

Since banks live by their words, Citibank will honor such a commitment, but an account officer who shows bad judgment in making lending decisions is unlikely to be employed for long. That is the safeguard against "policy violations," and it is a most effective one. Parenthetically, it is worth pointing out that all Citibank loans are made by account officers. Citibank does not make "front office" loans.

IV — Banking for Government

State And Municipal Bonds: It is true that Citibank holds a relatively small proportion of its assets in state and municipal securities. That is a business decision which, in the light of recent market conditions, we have had no cause to regret. Balancing earnings potential and the degree of risk involved, there is a wide variety of possible uses for investable funds. It is utter nonsense, therefore, to suggest that we would be more heavily invested in state and municipal securities were it not for our role in aircraft leasing. These are not the alternatives.

In arguing for the issuance of subsidized state and local debt instruments in fully-taxable form, the Nader report essentially recognized that the market cannot be expected to buy governmental securities unless they pay a satisfactory rate of return. Yet this section also argues that Citibank is neglecting its civic duty by failing to buy or hold more governmental securities than its management regards as wise. We suggest that these two arguments are in direct contradiction.

New York City Checking Accounts: This section is incorrect in several particulars and misleading in others. It says, for example, that "a few of the large banks have expressed displeasure" over New York City's shift to a zero balance system (page 137). We do not know the attitudes of other banks, but we have always expressed the view that the city's pool and satellite or zero balance system was highly efficient and represented a desirable development from the City's standpoint.

Indeed, some time before New York City adopted its own system, Citibank's Corporate Cash Management unit had already developed and begun marketing a similar program called ACT. Obviously, Citibank would not and could not have discouraged a potential user from employing a concept compatible with our own program. Furthermore, the fact is that we use the ACT program in administering the City's pool and satellite system.

According to Citibank's ledger and other activities analysis employing cost figures, which we believe to be considerably more accurate than those cited in the Nader report, our direct charges for handling of New York City accounts were $1.3 million, not $880,000.

And our annual income before allocation of costs of credit, financial and other advisory services was $1.48 million, not $2.25 million. Moreover, these additional costs ignored by the analysis cited in the Nader report amounted to some $400,000. Thus, in actual fact, our costs were about $1.7 million and our profit was approximately $1.1 million.

	Nader figures	Citibank figures
Average Investable Balance	$48,214,000	$42,827,000
Gross Annual Income	3,134,000	2,797,000
Ledger and Other Activity Analysis Charges	880,000	1,315,000
Income before allocation of costs of credit, financial and other advisory services	2,254,000	1,482,000
Additional Services	—	400,000
Profit	2,254,000	1,082,000

It should be noted further that in 1969, Citibank served as clearing bank during the final quarter of the year, which resulted in unusually high balances, and that the Treasury Bill rate used in calculating gross annual income was at 6.5 percent, an unusually high rate. In 1971, the Treasury Bill rate was 4.41 percent. Despite these abnormal circumstances, Citibank's profit/expense ratio was 73 percent, not 256 percent as alleged by the Nader report.

All such figures are incomplete, however, because they necessarily ignore factors in the relationship between Citibank and New York City which are not susceptible to statistical analysis.

These include our efforts to help the City devise a solution to the welfare check distribution problem, our participation in the food stamp program, our long-time role in the City's financing efforts, our work in making a market for the City's financial obligations and the contributions of the bank's regional economics section in analyzing the City's economic and social problems.

That section recently authored a book, *Profile of a City*, that was published by McGraw-Hill Company.

In summary, we believe that New York City gets excellent service at a fair price from Citibank and we emphatically deny the allegation that we have earned exorbitant profits from handling the City's accounts.

Pension Fund Advisory Service: Typical of the Nader report's tendency to condemn or misinterpret any service rendered by Citibank is its indictment of Citibank's service without fee as advisor on $2.7 billion of bonds and $105 million of stocks in the municipal employee pension fund.

The report quotes the New York City Comptroller's office (page 136) as stating that Citibank has done " an excellent job" and that income has been increased by about $15 million per year as a result of changes made with the advice of Citibank and the other advisors.

It is alleged, however, that Citibank may have "wanted the job" to attract deposits for the bank from brokers.

The fact is that during the approximately two years that Citibank had been advising the Comptroller without charging a fee, total bond transactions initiated by Citibank with brokers of our choice involved $6 million face value of bonds. All other transactions were initiated directly by the Comptroller's office without consultation with Citibank as to the choice of broker-dealer. Not a single one of the FNCB-initiated orders was placed with Halsey Stuart. (See page 348 and pages 361-2 of Nader text and pages 5 and 11 of the Citibank statement.)

Alleged Conflicts: The report discusses at length the circumstances surrounding the service of Eben W. Pyne, a senior vice president of Citibank on the special committee appointed by Governor Rockefeller in 1964 to make recommendations concerning the Long Island Railroad and subsequently on the Metropolitan Transportation Authority created by New York State in 1967.

It should be pointed out, first of all, that Mr. Pyne's appointment to the MTA following State purchase of the LIRR was made with the advice and consent of the New York State Senate after consideration by the Senate's finance committee.

Although Mr. Pyne's affiliation with Citibank was well known, no conflict of interest charges were raised, and for good reason, because there was no conflict. Mr. Pyne has scrupulously complied with his responsibilities under Section 73 of the Public Officers Law, the statute dealing with conflict of interest.

The special committee's recommendation that New York State buy the LIRR from the Pennsylvania Railroad for $65 million is characterized by Nader as a "giveaway."

The facts are that the Pennsylvania wanted $116 million for the LIRR, that the cost of condemnation was estimated at $250 million and that construction of capacity to move an equivalent 260,000 commuters into and out of New York City daily on a highway-tunnel network was estimated at $2 billion.

The $65 million purchase price recommended by the special committee, as well as necessary modernization of the lines, was agreed to by both houses of the New York State Legislature. The opposing arguments summarized by the Nader report were considered and rejected.

The report also attempts to raise suspicions regarding the takeover by the States of New York and Connecticut of New Haven railroad commuter operations from the Penn Central. As in the case of the LIRR, the primary concern was the preservation of commuter service which, as the report acknowledges, was operating at an annual loss of $6 million to $8 million a year.

The facts concerning Citibank's relations with Penn Central relative to this matter are important. Citibank participated to the extent of $35 million in a $300 million loan commitment entered into with Penn Central 21 months prior to the takeover of the New Haven in Januray, 1971. Citibank's participation in the loan commitment amounted to less than 12 percent of the total.

Finally, the report alleges (page 150ff) that Mr. Pyne voted to raise New York City transit fares from 20 cents to 30 cents so as not to tap the city's revenues, thus weakening security for bonds held by the banks.

Once again the report omits a material fact, namely that Mr. Pyne and other MTA members appealed unsuccessfully to Mayor Lindsay for a general revenue subsidy in order to avoid the fare increase.

It also neglects to mention that New York City bonds are secured by the unlimited taxing powers of the City and that bondholders have first lien on the City's revenues before any other payout. Thus, the notion that Mr. Pyne favored a fare increase to protect bonds held by Citibank is false.

The World Trade Center: This section confuses fact and opinion in such a way as to create inferences which are inaccurate. For example, we know of no evidence to substantiate the statement (page 141) that "the banks, through the Downtown Lower Manhattan Association, conceived the World Trade Center."

It is true that the DLMA played a significant part in the conception and sponsorship of the World Trade Center and that major New York banks were represented on the DLMA board. The reader is invited to infer that DLMA represented the banks and was in effect their agency. A more accurate picture would show that the banks did not have a majority position on the DLMA board.

The essential truth is that a number of New York business interests supported construction of the World Trade Center as a means of preserving New York City's leadership position in international trade.

New York City banks agreed to help finance it, partly as a business venture and partly because, as New York residents, they shared in the desire to revitalize the City's economic base.

Home Mortgages: The section dealing with home mortgages is off the point. The report ignores the fact that Citibank has the largest FHA mortgage portfolio of any commercial bank in the country.

But the U.S. Congress has created an entire class of savings and loan institutions to provide residential mortgage financing and has given those institutions a favored position in competing for savings accounts as well as a privileged tax status. Commercial banks generally are therefore not in position to compete on an economic basis in residential mortgage financing.

Citibank has made clear on many occasions that it would welcome a change in national policy permitting greater across-the-board competition between commercial banks and other depository institutions.

Instead of addressing itself meaningfully to the the issue of competition between commercial banks and savings institutions, the Nader report simply berates Citibank for declining to sacrifice better profit opportunities and the Federal Reserve Board for not requiring commercial banks to subsidize the housing market. The report's quarrel here, as elsewhere, is with national policy, and its criticism of Citibank is entirely misdirected.

V — In Citibank We Trust

Citibank's responses to the Nader study group allegations about investment in and voting of Citicorp stock, relations between the trust department and commercial side of the bank, the IMG's investment performance, investment in director-affiliated companies, uninvested cash balances, research methodology and broker reciprocity are found in Mr. Wriston's statement. (Pages 8-12.)

Portfolio Turnovers: The report alleges (page 178) that "there is the temptation for the bank once it has gotten the business, to ignore the trust altogether since the settlor is dead."

Personal trust accounts managed by the bank are regularly reviewed by the account manager and, in addition, every account is individually examined once a year by the personal trust investment committee.

In those instances where there has been no change in the individual's investment portfolio, that fact represents a deliberate decision resulting from the investor's particular circumstances — e.g., advanced age of the beneficiary, low tax base, etc. — which in our judgment make a portfolio change inadvisable.

Common Trust Funds: These are an investment vehicle (page 180ff) for smaller trust accounts. As compared to individually managed trust accounts, CTFs provide both more diversified and flexible portfolio management than would be available at comparable fees to an individual trust in the $50,000 to $250,000 range. Citibank maintains the following four discretionary CTFs:

Fund A — Income-Oriented Equity Fund
Fund B — Taxable-Fixed Income Fund
Fund C — Growth-Oriented Equity Fund
Fund D — Tax-Exempt Municipal Bond Fund

Through a combination of the four discretionary CTFs, it is possible to tailor each individual participation so as to meet the specific needs of beneficiaries of a particular trust.

The advantages of the CTFs are such that many trusts with assets substantially in excess of $250,000 may also benefit from full or partial investment in CTF participations. CTFs are a fiduciary medium explicitly recognized under New York and Connecticut laws which govern the bulk of the trusts administered by Citibank.

Depending on the terms of the trust agreement, certain "foreign" trusts may also be eligible for participation in CTFs. Altogether, the four CTFs administered by Citibank represent a small fraction of the total assets managed by the personal trust department, which in turn manages only a portion of the total assets handled by the Investment Management Group.

IMG has undertaken the transfer of most smaller individual trust accounts into one or more of the bank's four CTFs, except where the duration of the trust, its current yield or other factors made a change inadvisable from the standpoint of the beneficiary. In those cases where consent of co-fiduciaries is required, Citibank seeks to persuade them that such a transfer would benefit the account. Most agree and appear satisfied with the results.

In a few cases, co-fiduciaries have refused to allow a transfer. Although not legally obligated to do so, Citibank has also consented to maintain individual accounts in certain cases where the beneficiaries were opposed to entering a common trust fund and could cite a persuasive reason for not doing so.

An audited financial report of each common trust fund is made annually to all CTF holders along with quarterly interim reports. In addition, a public accounting is made in New York Surrogate's Court every four years. Thus, participants in the CTFs have every opportunity to state their views to the bank as trustee and to pursue any complaints they may have about performance.

Pension Fund Holdings in Employer's Stock: Citibank's rules regarding purchase of stock in the employing corporation for a profit sharing or pension fund account attempt to recognize the fact that circumstances vary.

What might be appropriate for one fund would not necessarily be appropriate for another. In some cases, the terms of the agreement setting up the fund — terms by which Citibank must abide — either forbid or require such investment.

Thus, one pension fund managed by Citibank bars any investment in securities issued by the employing corporation although that corporation has been extremely successful over the years. Citibank has great confidence in the firm's stock and has purchased it for nearly every pension account it manages except the pension fund of the issuing corporation.

On the other hand, the terms of another employee benefit account, a profit sharing fund, require that a portion of the assets of the fund must be invested in the employer's stock.

Problems arise primarily when the employing corporation's stock is not a particularly high-rated investment. In general, where discretion rests wholly with the IMG, Citibank's rule provides that an investment in the employer's stock may be made only if it is on the recommended buy list for other accounts.

Under such circumstances, Citibank regards investment in the employer's stock, in proportions similar to its representation in other employee benefit accounts, as fully consistent with a prudent investment policy.

In the case of pension fund accounts where co-trustees have the right under the trust agreement to direct the bank to purchase the employer's securities and where those securities are not on the recommended buy list for other accounts, the bank will allow such purchases only up to a maximum of five per cent of total fund assets.

Profit sharing or thrift-savings plans which are set up under agreements requiring a proportion of the assets to be invested in the employer's stock are not, of course, subject to this limitation.

Citibank believes it would be unwise to adopt any general requirement forbidding investment of every type of employee benefit funds in securities of the employing corporation. In view of the variety of circumstances encountered, Citibank thinks such a universal prohibition would be harmful since it would preclude application of individual tests to particular cases. The bank's own rules, it believes, allow for a fair balance to be struck between potential profitability and prudence.

Campaign GM: In 1971 Citibank voted against the independent stockholder proposals advanced at the annual meeting of the General Motors Corporation. Before this decision was made, the proposals advanced by Campaign GM and the Episcopal Church's Committee on Social Criteria for Investments were carefully considered by our Investment Policy Committee.

The committee came to the conclusion that two of the proposals were meritorious in concept but impractical as framed. Accordingly, in communicating its decision to GM management, Citibank indicated its desire to see additional disclosure by GM management on matters of corporate and social responsibility and also urged GM to take an open-minded approach to the selection of candidates for the corporation's board of directors so as to assure that the board would be responsive to legitimate concerns of shareholders.

The discussion on pages 210-11 of the Nader report is incorrect in asserting that Citibank simply went along with management.

VI — Bank Regulation

This part of the report is less a criticism of Citibank than of the bank regulatory agencies, which are more than competent to defend themselves. We can only say for ourselves that the view that Citibank is essentially unregulated or that it has "captured" the regulatory agencies is completely out of touch with reality.

The fact that Citibank tries to make its views known to the regulatory agencies and that sometimes our advice is heeded by no means alters the basic situation, which is that banking suffers from an excess of regulation which has tended to clothe anti-competitive actions in pro-competitive rhetoric.

The Nader report, in this section, is guilty of the latter fault when it urges policies that would shelter portions of the financial market from effective competition by commercial banks.

Insofar as they deal specifically with Citibank, we wish to make the following points regarding the chapter on bank regulation:

National Advisory Committee: At the time that George S. Moore, Citibank's former chairman who retired in 1970 before the Nader study was started, was also chairman of the National Advisory Committee to the Comptroller of the Currency, Congress passed a law making it a crime for anyone knowingly to make a false statement "for the purpose of influencing in any way the action of . . . any bank . . . insured by the Federal Deposit Insurance Corporation."

The Nader book cites this as a good example of "the bankers' power to obtain self-serving legislation" and credits Mr. Moore with being "the prime mover behind this law" (page 283).

What the report fails to point out is that the 1970 act was an amendment to earlier legislation which already made it a crime to make a false statement to a Federal savings and loan association, a Federal land bank association, a small business investment company, a Federal credit union and a number of government institutions.

The 1970 amendment added banks insured by the FDIC, but it also added State-chartered credit unions, any institution insured by the Federal Savings and Loan Insurance Corporation and any member of the Federal Home Loan Bank System.

Thus, it was not an amendment for banks only, as the Nader book implies, nor was it a novel concept. The NAC viewed the omission of federally insured institutions from the earlier law as illogical. The Comptroller agreed, and so did the Congress.

In view of these facts, it seems clear that the quotation from the NAC minutes ("Chairman Moore felt that some corrective legislation was needed in this area") hardly sustains the study group's conclusion that Mr. Moore was "the prime mover behind this law."

Bank Examinations: While the criticisms in this section are chiefly directed at the Comptroller of the Currency, Citibank must point out that the bank maintains a full-time audit staff of approximately 275 people and that, in addition, Citibank is audited annually by an independent accounting firm.

Furthermore, like other large banks, Citibank makes many loans to public corporations, which in turn publish independently audited financial statements.

It is for these reasons that examinations of Citibank and other large banks lend themselves to much more of a sampling procedure than can be employed in the case of smaller institutions. Therefore, comparisons based on asset size are irrelevant.

We reject as outrageous the comment (page 290) that the training program for bank examiners in electronic data processing on which Peat, Marwick & Mitchell assisted "is a clear conflict of interest." The implication that Citibank and Peat, Marwick might be conspiring to control the Comptroller's examination procedures manages simultaneously to question Citibank's honesty, Peat, Marwick's ethics and the Comptroller's intelligence.

We wonder whether, as lawyers, the members of Mr. Nader's study group will consider themselves to have conflicts of interest if they are ever asked to serve on public advisory bodies or on bar association committees dealing with subject matter that also happens to concern one or more of their clients.

Cooperation With The Fed: It is incorrect to contend (page 305ff) that Citibank failed to cooperate with the objectives of the Federal Reserve Board in restraining credit during 1969. Obviously, lines of credit that were outstanding at the time could not be precipitously withdrawn without defaulting on our obligations to customers.

However, as the year progressed and as the Fed stepped up its efforts to restrict the rate of growth on loans, Citibank reduced the rate of growth of its loans accordingly. Overall, Citibank reduced its loan-to-deposit ratios in about the same proportion as the "average" U.S. bank and made a slightly larger percentage reduction than the average of all banks in New York.

Citibank's innovative role in the creation of the negotiable certificates of deposit and in the development of the Eurodollar market is well known, but is misinterpreted and inaccurately described in the Nader book.

Eurodollar transactions were employed by FNCB and other banks during 1969-70 in order to gain some flexibility in adjusting to conditions in U.S. financial markets. But this process took place under the Federal Reserve Board's watchful eye and under its periodic guidance.

In August, 1969, the Fed imposed a 10 percent marginal reserve requirement on Eurodollar transfers to New York above each bank's average holdings in May 1969.

When Citibank in October, 1970, indicated its intention

of reducing its Eurodollar takings, thus reducing its reserve-free "base", the Fed indicated a desire for money center banks to preserve their basic Eurodollar position so as not to disturb the balance of payments which had been improved by the Eurodollar transfers. Citibank, of course, complied with the Fed's request.

The notion that banks managed to "evade" the monetary design of the Federal Reserve Board through access to the Eurodollar market is groundless. The fact that the Fed did not always forsee the consequences of its actions — which is the only implication of the exchange between Messrs. Exter and Laeri quoted in the Nader report (page 308), does not mean that the Fed was powerless or that Citibank merrily went its own way.

On the contrary, Citibank's stake as a money center bank in the successful operation of the system provides a strong incentive for Citibank to be responsive to the wishes of the Fed and, as often happens, to alert the Fed to problems and trends which may not yet have become apparent.

One-Bank Holding Companies: The burden of the section on the one-bank holding company legislation of 1970 (**page 315ff**) is that Mr. Nader's associates disagree with the action of the U.S. Congress. That is certainly their privilege.

As to the facts, Citibank organized as a bank holding company in 1968 as a part of an attempt to broaden the range of financial services which it could offer to meet what we perceived as unfilled marketplace needs.

We do not feel required to defend our efforts to persuade Congress to enact legislation which would preserve the flexibility which the holding company technique affords. We simply exercised the rights available to us under the law and the Constitution to make our views known to Congress.

The law that eventually passed was not entirely in keeping with our wishes, nor have we obviously agreed in every case with the Federal Reserve Board's decisions in administering the law.

48

Nader Appendices

Summary of Recommendations: As indicated elsewhere in this response, many of the recommendations in the book simply do not apply, either because they are addressed to conditions which have been corrected under Citibank's regular program of self-examination and self-improvement or because they deal with nonexistent problems (e.g., the recommendation that the trust department be prohibited from exercising voting control over its own stock).

Rebuttal and Surrebuttal: We see no point to adding a counter-surrebuttal. We find it interesting, however, that despite the strenuous insistence of the study group that it made no errors in the initial report, many of the sweeping allegations criticized in our original response have been softened or eliminated.

Except in the surrebuttal, for example, the study group no longer insists that, despite our denials, we employed commissions from New York City's pension fund to attract broker deposits. The report now merely "wonder(s) . . . whether Citibank wanted the job to use the power to choose brokers as a device to attract deposits from those brokers" (page 136).

The study group is now speculating baselessly instead of accusing falsely. From our standpoint, that is no improvement.

III-Citibank Appendices

Citibank Appendix One

The Nader group alleges that Mr. Wriston ordered Citibank staff members not to talk to his task force. This was not the case. Here are all of the memos to the Citibank staff issued by Mr. Wriston which clearly show that no such instruction was given.

MEMORANDUM TO: All Officers
RE: *Nader Project*

As you are undoubtedly aware, Mr. Ralph Nader met with Bill Spencer and me yesterday. Mr. Nader said that, while he had no fault to find with Citibank, the time had come to learn how a large financial institution operates. To that end, he wants to send in a team to roam the Bank.

We pointed out to Mr. Nader that Citibank shares his concern for the consumer, but that Citibank people have a responsibility to protect their customers from invasions of their privacy.

We explained to Mr. Nader that after all, Citibank invented the personal loan as a way to protect New Yorkers from loan sharks. We have pioneered such consumer services as the home improvement loan. We are the nation's leader in student loans as well as a considerable participant in attempts to solve this City's problems.

We also called Mr. Nader's attention to Citibank's deep concern with the growing invasion of the individual's right to privacy, for Bill Spencer and Ralph Nader both serve on the National Advisory Panel of the Project on Computer Data Banks. This is a study program sponsored by the National Academy of Science and is funded by the Russell Sage Foundation. It seeks ways of protecting the individual from any incursions that the computer could make into his right to privacy.

We told Mr. Nader that, of course, he could expect to receive the same information that any other responsible individual or member of the press is entitled to. We concluded our meeting with the promise to discuss the matter with the banking group heads and to get in touch with him.

Consequently, we expect to tell Mr. Nader that we would be willing to have him interview the group heads just as members of responsible publications like *Fortune* and *Business Week* have interviewed Citibankers. And in order to avoid misunderstanding, these interviews will be tape recorded.

Our customers' affairs are private and we have an obligation to protect the individual's constitutional right to privacy. Indeed, this obligation has been upheld on numerous occasions by the courts. Under no circumstances, therefore, can we permit Mr. Nader's assistants to roam the Bank at will.

To avoid confusion, I have asked Don Colen, or Lamson Smith in his absence, to serve as a point of coordination. Refer any inquiries from Mr. Nader, his assistants or the press to Don. After all, we have a business to run and by coordinating our responses, we can maintain perspective and prevent the disruption of our basic priority which is to serve our customers as capably as we know how.

Walter B. Wriston
Chairman

June 16, 1970

MEMORANDUM TO: All Officers
             RE: Nader Project

This is in the nature of a progress report. Since my memorandum of June 16, two lengthy conferences have been held with Mr. David Leinsdorf, head of the Nader task force assigned to the bank. Mr. Leinsdorf is a graduate of Columbia Law School and, for the past 2½ years, has been associated with the U.S. District Attorney's Office here in New York. His team will probably consist of 10-12 first-year law students attending Columbia, N.Y.U., Harvard and Yale. Howard Laeri, Vice Chairman, and Don Colen, Vice President, have been conducting our meetings with Mr. Leinsdorf. At my request, Mr. Laeri is now the senior officer in charge of the project for the bank. In his absence, Carl Desch, Senior Vice President and Cashier, will serve as alternate.

Alhtough Mr. Leinsdorf is unable at this time to spell out the objectives of his study, he did submit a blanket request covering numerous documents, policy memoranda and so forth. We have reviewed these requests against the background of the original guidelines which were set. These, you will recall, were:

1) We will cooperate with Mr. Nader's project and provide his group with the same information that we would give to any stockholder or member of the working press.
2) We have an obligation to maintain our customers' right to privacy.
3) We will not disclose information which would damage our competitive position.

Using these criteria, we have gone over the list of requests and will deliver to Mr. Leinsdorf today all documents which may be released consistent with these principles. For your information, the list of documents which we delivered to Mr. Leinsdorf is attached. This list does not fulfill all of Mr. Leinsdorf's requests because some documents were withheld to protect the privacy of individuals and for competitive reasons.

You will recall that we offered to arrange interviews with the Banking Group Heads with the understanding that such interviews would be tape recorded so that there would be no misunderstanding, and that a representative designated by Mr. Laeri would be present at all such interviews. Mr. Leinsdorf has not yet told us the names of the people who are working on the Nader task force, but we hope to have this information shortly.

Mr. Leinsdorf has recently indicated that he has in mind having his people conduct as many as 750 interviews with bank officers and employees of his selection. Naturally, since we have a bank to run, Mr. Leinsdorf has been told that we could not agree to the degree of disruption that such massive incursions of our time would create. As an alternative, we have asked that he submit a list of what he considers to be priority interviews, and we will then do our best to accommodate ourselves to any reasonable program. It is our impression that Mr. Leinsdorf plans to have his team concentrate its interviewing process largely on the younger officers of the bank. This is fine and, to the extent that we can cooperate, we plan to do so.

We have an understanding with Mr. Leinsdorf that we will arrange all appointments. Therefore, in the interest of orderly procedure, we ask that none of you grant interviews unless officially requested to do so by Messrs. Laeri, Desch or Colen. Mr. Leinsdorf has pointed out to us that his men are largely inexperienced in interviewing and in the banking business and that fact should be borne in mind.

If you are one of those designated to meet a member of the Nader task force, you must, of course, be guided by ground rules that I outlined earlier. Beyond that, we request your cooperation within reasonable time limits. As was stated in my memorandum of June 16, our basic priority is the bank's day-to-day business and serving our customers as capably as we can.

Walter B. Wriston
Chairman

July 3, 1970

Documents Furnished to Mr. David Leinsdorf
(Numbers correspond to items on the initial list of documents submitted by Mr. Leinsdorf on June 23, 1970).

1. Organization Chart of First National City Corporation showing consolidated subsidiaries.

2. Administrative Directories for Jan/1970 and Mar/1969, and "Meet the Innovators" directory for the Corporate Banking Group.

3. Various press releases, quarterly and annual reports to stockholders, public statements of officers, reports on city environment, and monthly economic newsletters.

4. Rules governing the extension of credit.

7. Memorandum of June 24, 1970, concerning First National City Bank in its urban environment.

9. Sample agreements for consumer loans.
   a. Note (Property Improvement, PBR 539 Rev. 12-69 FHA Note).
   b. Note (Personal Finance Department, PBR 583 Rev. 2-70).
   c. Note (Personal Finance Department, PSF 608 Rev. 3-70 — Payroll Deduction Plan).
   d. Collateralized Note (Personal Finance Department, PBR 662 Rev. 11-69 — with assignment of wages).
   e. Collateralized Note (Personal Finance Department, PBR 663 Rev. 5-69 — without assignment of wages).
   f. Note (Personal Finance Department, PBR 664 Coop. Apt. Financing 1-70).
   g. Collateralized Note (Personal Finance Department PSF 723 Rev. 11-69—Payroll Deduction with assignment of wages).

h. Security Agreement (Retail Installment Contract, PDL 590 Rev. 10-69).
i. Note (PDL 570 Rev. 3-70), together with Retail Installment Obligation (PDL 569 Rev. 11-69 (FHA)).
j. Notice of Right to Rescind Transaction with respect to Retail Installment Obligation (PBR 661 Rev. 11-69).
k. Agreement and Note for Student Loan (PBR 639 Rev. 9-69), together with Disclosure Statement (PSF 713 Rev. 3/70).
l. Citibank's forms for loan plan for New York Higher Education Assistance Corporation (Affidavit of Residence in New York State (HE 1150 7/67), Interim Promissory Note — (In School) (HE 700 9/69), Promissory Note — Installment (HE 800 1/70), Disclosure Statement of Loan (PSF 722 6-69), Student's Application and Application for Renewal/Repayment of Student Loan (PSF 626 Rev. 5-70).
m. Security Agreement (Chattel Mortgage) (PSF 576 Rev. 5-65).
n. Assignment of Life Insurance Policy as Collateral (SF 1924 (L) Rev. 1-65).
o. Assignment of (Mutual Fund) Shares (PCR 551 Rev. 7-64).
p. Master Charge Retail Installment Credit Agreement and Terms and Conditions of Use.
q. Ready-Credit/Checking-Plus Disclosure Statement (PRL 623 Rev. 8-69 (S)).

11. Sample Agreements.
a. Master Charge Service Seller's Agreement (CHS 543 Rev. 1-70).
b. Accounts Receivable Financing Volume Plan (Personal Finance Department, Time Contracts Section) and related forms.

c. Assignment of Accounts Receivable (SF 2019 (L) Rev. 11-64).

d. Letter-Agreements (two forms) re: Loans Secured by Accounts Receivable (Time Contracts Section).

e. Factoring Agreement (Hubshman Factors Department, HF 527B (L) Rev. 10-67).

f. Financing Agreement (Factoring and Commercial Finance Department, HF 527 (L) Rev. 4-69).

14. FNCB Capital Corporation brochure.

16. Citibank country studies on Argentina, Morocco, Japan and the Central American Common Market.

20. Press releases, Citibank News, Citibank Magazine and other news and magazine articles re: Street Academy, Canal Street Training Center and other similar programs, December 1969 correspondent bank seminar statements on employment policies and Working Together brochure.

22. Application Forms

a. Application for Residential Mortgage Loan.

   (i) FHA Mortgage Agreement (MRE 506 AR Rev. 7-69).

   (ii) Mortgage Agreement (MRE 506R (L) Rev. 7-69).

   (iii) Appraisal Report (MRE 501 6-65).

   (iv) Disclosures Required Under Federal Law (MRE — 593 6-69).

   (v) Mortgage Note (MRE 533 (L) Rev. 4-69).

   (vi) Mortgage-N.Y. (MRE 527 (L) Rev. 8-67).

   (vii) Mortgage-N.J. (MRE 564 (L) Rev. 8-68).

b. Application for Personal Loan (PBR 579 Rev. 10-69 Personal (Signature) Loan).

c. Application for Personal Loan (PBR 633 Rev. 10/69 — Auto. Boat. Prop. Mod. Collat. & Spec. Adv.).

d. Applications for Property Improvement Loan (PDL 580 Rev. 10-69), (PBR 538 Rev. 10-69 FHA Branch), and (PDL 518 Rev. 10-69 FHA Dealer).

e. Application for Personal Loan—Payroll Deduction Plan (PSF 639 Rev. 10-69).

f. Application for Personal Loan (PDL 575 Rev. 6-69 Personal (Signature Loan — Sec. 108 Premium & Travel).

g. Application for Travel Loan (PSF 694 Rev. 6-69).

h. Application for Personal Loan (and Note) to pay for professional services.

i. Buyer's Statement (for purchase of vehicle) (PSF 665A Rev. 10-69).

j. Application for Equipment Lease (corporation). (PSF 677 Rev. 11-64).

k. Application for Monthly Payment Business Loan (Partnership or corporation) (PBR 635 Rev. 4-69 MPB Loan).

l. Application, Commercial Modernization, C&I Improvement (PSF 605 Rev. 8-67).

m. Physician/Dentist Business Loan Application (PBR 646 Rev. 1-69).

n. Checking Plus Application (Borrower's Statement) (PRC 617 Rev. 12-69).

o. Application — Ready-Credit (PRC 507 Rev. 6-69).

p. Master Charge Application (CHS 547 Rev. 7-69), with Retail Installment Credit Agreement attached.

23. Minutes of annual meetings of stockholders for years 1968-70.

27. Affirmative Action Program, June 1969, together with statement on non-discrimination and form of employment application.

MEMORANDUM TO: All Citibankers

Mr. Ralph Nader called me today. He asked whether we would again grant interviews with Citibankers so that his group could now restudy the operations of the Investment Management Group.

You will recall that the last time Nadermen were in the bank, we complied with their request for personal interviews with 53 Citibank officers, and countless telephone interviews, stretching out over a period of months. Included at that time were five interviews with senior officers of the Investment Management Group.

Our efforts to cooperate with Mr. Nader's young law students required nearly a year of Citibank time, and we have estimated that Citibank spent nearly 10,000 man-hours on this project.

When the interviews were completed and the law students left to write their book, there was no indication that the project was only partially completed and that the students expected to conduct additional interviews. Certainly we had not agreed to a two-stage process.

The Nader report, as it was published, reflected very little of what the students had learned in the interviews. We had hoped that we would learn from their fresh insights. Instead we were disappointed to find the report was filled with inaccuracies, distortions and misconceptions, and was based largely on other often fragmentary material, including what other people had written about the bank from time to time.

We don't think we can justify another such unproductive expense to our stockholders. And in view of the uneven quality of the report, we don't think either Citibank's or the public's interest would be served by another such undertaking.

Therefore, we are turning down Mr. Nader's request.

October 4, 1971

Walter B. Wriston
Chairman

Citibank Appendix Two

Far from being shrouded in secrecy, Citibank's Investment Management Group pioneered in disclosing pertinent details on its holdings, voting authority, and buying and selling operations. This is the fourth year that such data has been made public in an annual report by the IMG. In this appendix, significant data on IMG's 1973 operations are presented.

DEGREE OF INVESTMENT DISCRETION

This table discloses the degree of investment discretion exercised by Citibank over the 100 largest common stock holdings in fiduciary accounts. This information follows and includes:

- Market value of holdings in all advisory and trust accounts.
- Market value of discretionary holdings, i.e. advisory accounts where the bank has power of attorney over the investments, trust accounts where the bank acts as sole or joint trustee with complete investment power.
- Discretionary holdings as a percentage of the company's total shares outstanding.
- The percentage each holding constitutes of all common stocks held in discretionary accounts.

These figures represent the most accurate way of measuring the degree of investment control Citibank holds in any single company and the degree to which the assets we manage are diversified among the many different companies.

DEGREE OF INVESTMENT DISCRETION

December 31, 1973

Issue	Total Fiduciary Holdings Market Value ($ Millions)	Discretionary Holdings		
		Market Value ($ Millions)	Percent of Outstanding Shares (%)	Percent of Total Discretionary Holdings (%)
1 International Business Machines Corporation	$832	$610	1.69%	9.26%
2 Xerox Corporation	590	478	4.92	7.25
3 Eastman Kodak Company	401	295	1.57	4.48
4 Merck & Co., Inc.	305	243	4.06	3.69
5 The Coca-Cola Company	282	228	3.01	3.46
6 General Electric Company	281	211	1.84	3.20
7 Johnson & Johnson	234	206	3.18	3.12
8 Atlantic Richfield Company	218	186	3.67	2.82
9 Minnesota Mining and Manufacturing Company	214	180	2.05	2.74
10 Exxon Corporation	206	107	.51	1.63
11 Avon Products, Inc.	198	168	4.55	2.55
12 Sears, Roebuck and Co.	193	143	1.13	2.17

Issue	Total Fiduciary Holdings Market Value ($ Millions)	Discretionary Holdings		
		Market Value ($ Millions)	Percent of Outstanding Shares (%)	Percent of Total Discretionary Holdings (%)
13 Texas Instruments Incorporated	172	143	5.88	2.17
14 J. C. Penney Company, Inc.	169	134	3.21	2.03
15 S. S. Kresge Company	165	143	3.72	2.17
16 Caterpillar Tractor Co.	163	143	3.72	2.16
17 Eli Lilly and Company	154	130	2.54	1.96
18 First National City Corporation†	133	24	.44	.37
19 General Motors Corporation	117	74	.56	1.13
20 Hewlett-Packard Company	104	94	4.35	1.43
21 Corning Glass Works	103	4	.33	.07
22 J. P. Morgan & Co. Incorporated	100	70	2.78	1.06
23 Texaco Inc.	95	15	.19	.23
24 Philip Morris Incorporated	83	72	2.29	1.09
25 American Hospital Supply Corporation	82	67	4.85	1.01

26	Motorola Inc.	77	71	5.22	1.08
27	Emerson Electric Co.	76	72	3.20	1.10
28	American Home Products Corporation	73	38	.60	.57
29	Schering-Plough Corporation	73	55	1.48	.84
30	General Telephone & Electronics Corporation	66	55	1.86	.83
31	Honeywell Inc.	63	53	3.98	.80
32	Sony Corporation	62	54	2.72	.82
33	E. I. du Pont de Nemours & Company	56	30	.39	.45
34	American Telephone and Telegraph Company	54	26	.09	.39
35	American Express Company	54	39	1.22	.59
36	Walt Disney Productions	49	43	3.09	.65
37	Westinghouse Electric Corporation	47	6	.26	.09
38	McDonald's Corporation	44	35	1.54	.53
39	Whirlpool Corporation	44	41	4.51	.62
40	Baxter Laboratories, Inc.	43	37	2.64	.56
41	AMP Incorporated	40	34	2.35	.51

†It is our policy to carry First National City Corporation stock in a customer's portfolio only upon receipt of his written instructions.

	Total Fiduciary Holdings Market Value ($ Millions)	Discretionary Holdings		
Issue		Market Value ($ Millions)	Percent of Outstanding Shares (%)	Percent of Total Discretionary Holdings (%)
42 The Bendix Corporation	40	*	.10	**
43 Mobil Oil Corporation	40	24	.45	.37
44 The Travelers Corporation	40	35	2.35	.53
45 Standard Oil Company (Indiana)	39	12	.17	.19
46 Virginia Electric and Power Company	38	33	4.53	.51
47 Colgate-Palmolive Company	37	*	.01	**
48 The Upjohn Company	37	24	1.11	.36
49 Ford Motor Company	36	32	.79	.48
50 The Perkin-Elmer Corporation	33	28	5.38	.42
51 The Southern Company	33	30	2.28	.45
52 Continental Telephone Corporation	31	28	4.50	.42
53 Union Oil Company of California	30	24	1.68	.36
54 Federated Department Stores, Inc.	30	25	1.99	.38

55	The Procter & Gamble Company	30	15	.20	.23
56	Digital Equipment Corporation	30	17	1.45	.26
57	TRW Inc.	28	28	6.07	.42
58	Chesebrough-Pond's Inc.	28	25	2.71	.37
59	First Chicago Corporation	28	21	1.53	.32
60	Florida Power & Light Company	27	20	2.38	.30
61	Texas Utilities	27	20	1.62	.31
62	Middle South Utilities, Inc.	27	24	3.24	.37
63	Moore Corporation Limited	26	25	1.66	.38
64	First International Bancshares, Inc.	26	21	2.90	.32
65	Doubleday & Company, Inc.	26	2	1.82	.02
66	The Chubb Corporation	25	3	.51	.05
67	Pennzoil Company	24	22	3.68	.34
68	United Telecommunications, Inc.	24	22	3.80	.33
69	Armstrong Cork Company	24	23	4.06	.35
70	Marcor Inc.	23	22	3.95	.33

Issue	Total Fiduciary Holdings Market Value ($ Millions)	Discretionary Holdings		
		Market Value ($ Millions)	Percent of Outstand- ing Shares (%)	Percent of Total Discretionary Holdings (%)
71 Textron Inc.	23	22	3.75	.34
72 Carolina Power & Light Company	23	18	3.75	.28
73 First Bank System, Inc.	22	21	2.45	.32
74 Matsushita Electric Industrial Co., Ltd.	22	20	1.26	.31
75 FMC Corporation	22	20	3.82	.31
76 Southern California Edison Company	22	21	2.51	.31
77 Commonwealth Edison Company	21	15	1.06	.23
78 Beatrice Foods Co.	20	18	1.11	.27
79 Schlumberger Limited	20	5	.11	.08
80 Consumers Power Company	19	6	1.08	.10
81 Standard Oil Company of California	19	10	.17	.15
82 Duke Power Company	18	11	1.62	.16
83 Marriott Corporation	18	15	2.56	.22
84 The Rank Organisation Limited	18	14	1.19	.21

85	Colonial Penn Group, Inc.	18	15	1.60	.22
86	The Hobart Manufacturing Company	18	0	0	0
87	Associated Dry Goods Corporation	17	17	4.82	.26
88	Economics Laboratory, Inc.	17	16	3.23	.24
89	The Louisiana Land and Exploration Company	16	7	.38	.11
90	General Mills, Inc.	16	12	.95	.19
91	Masco Corporation	16	13	2.61	.20
92	The National Cash Register Company	16	13	1.73	.19
93	Oklahoma Gas and Electric Company	15	14	3.39	.21
94	General Reinsurance Corporation	14	12	1.10	.19
95	The Lubrizol Corporation	14	12	1.64	.19
96	Northern Indiana Public Service Company	14	13	3.46	.19
97	Standard Oil Company (Ohio)	14	2	.08	.03
98	International Flavors and Fragrances, Inc.	14	9	.61	.13
99	Southern Pacific Company	14	12	1.15	.19
100	The Dow Chemical Company	14	4	.08	.06

Source for outstanding shares—Standard & Poor's Corporation Year-End 1973 Stock Guide.
*Less than $.5 million
**Less than .01%

VOTING AUTHORITY

This list includes common stock holdings in trust and advisory accounts, but not securities held on a strictly custodial basis. The ranking is by market value as of 12/31/73. The IMG's holdings in fiduciary accounts, and its voting authority over these shares, are expressed as percentages of the company's latest reported outstanding common stock.

The categories of voting authority are:

Sole — The bank alone is responsible for voting the shares.

Shared — The bank shares the voting responsibilities with a co-trustee or co-executor.

No — The bank has no voting authority and all proxies are mailed directly to the beneficial owners or to the parties exercising investment control.

VOTING AUTHORITY
December 31, 1973

Issue	Market Value ($ Millions)	Percent of Outstanding Shares			Total Fiduciary Holdings (%)
		Sole Voting (%)	Shared Voting (%)	No Voting (%)	
1 International Business Machines Corporation	$832	1.45%	.09%	.77%	2.31%
2 Xerox Corporation	590	4.22	.12	1.73	6.07
3 Eastman Kodak Company	401	1.37	.06	.70	2.14
4 Merck & Co., Inc.	305	3.29	.21	1.60	5.10
5 The Coca-Cola Company	282	2.90	.06	.76	3.73
6 General Electric Company	281	1.64	.06	.75	2.44
7 Johnson & Johnson	234	2.60	.03	1.00	3.62
8 Atlantic Richfield Company	218	3.29	.04	.98	4.31
9 Minnesota Mining and Manufacturing Company	214	1.75	.02	.65	2.43
10 Exxon Corporation	206	.52	.07	.39	.98
11 Avon Products, Inc.	198	3.84	.05	1.47	5.36
12 Sears, Roebuck and Co.	193	.94	.05	.54	1.53
13 Texas Instruments Incorporated	172	5.41	*	1.62	7.04

Percent of Outstanding Shares

Issue	Market Value ($ Millions)	Sole Voting (%)	Shared Voting (%)	No Voting (%)	Total Fiduciary Holdings (%)
14 J. C. Penney Company, Inc.	169	2.64	.06	1.34	4.04
15 S. S. Kresge Company	165	2.95	.03	1.31	4.29
16 Caterpillar Tractor Co.	163	3.58	.05	.62	4.25
17 Eli Lilly and Company	154	2.01	.04	.96	3.01
18 First National City Corporation	133	0	0	2.40	2.40
19 General Motors Corporation	117	.47	.06	.36	.89
20 Hewlett-Packard Company	104	4.06	0	.72	4.79
21 Corning Glass Works	103	.22	.27	7.24	7.73
22 J. P. Morgan & Co. Incorporated	100	2.40	.14	1.42	3.96
23 Texaco Inc.	95	.36	.04	.78	1.19
24 Philip Morris Incorporated	83	.67	*	1.97	2.64
25 American Hospital Supply Corporation	82	3.60	.05	2.32	5.98
26 Motorola Inc.	77	4.50	*	1.13	5.63

27	Emerson Electric Co.	76	3.17	*	.21	3.38
28	American Home Products Corporation	73	.46	.06	.65	1.17
29	Schering-Plough Corporation	73	1.09	.03	.84	1.96
30	General Telephone & Electronics Corporation	66	1.67	.03	.52	2.23
31	Honeywell Inc.	63	3.38	.05	1.26	4.70
32	Sony Corporation	62	2.39	.04	.71	3.14
33	E. I. du Pont de Nemours & Company	56	.17	.09	.48	.74
34	American Telephone and Telegraph Company	54	.08	.01	.11	.20
35	American Express Company	54	.94	.01	.74	1.70
36	Walt Disney Productions	49	2.56	.02	.89	3.48
37	Westinghouse Electric Corporation	47	.26	.01	1.83	2.10
38	McDonald's Corporation	44	1.25	.05	.65	1.96
39	Whirlpool Corporation	44	3.41	.02	1.39	4.82
40	Baxter Laboratories, Inc.	43	2.16	.01	.91	3.08
41	AMP Incorporated	40	1.83	0	.99	2.81
42	The Bendix Corporation	40	.01	.02	13.05	13.08
43	Mobil Oil Corporation	40	.44	.04	.27	.75

	Market Value ($ Millions)	Percent of Outstanding Shares				Total Fiduciary Holdings (%)
Issue		Sole Voting (%)	Shared Voting (%)	No Voting (%)		
44 The Travelers Corporation	40	2.44	.03	.23		2.69
45 Standard Oil Company (Indiana)	39	.19	.02	.34		.55
46 Virginia Electric and Power Company	38	3.35	.07	1.78		5.20
47 Colgate-Palmolive Company	37	.01	.01	2.16		2.17
48 The Upjohn Company	37	1.06	.02	.66		1.73
49 Ford Motor Company	36	.69	*	.20		.90
50 The Perkin-Elmer Corporation	33	4.71	.17	1.56		6.44
51 The Southern Company	33	1.85	.01	.69		2.55
52 Continental Telephone Corporation	31	3.93	.05	1.00		4.98
53 Union Oil Company of California	30	1.69	*	.44		2.13
54 Federated Department Stores, Inc.	30	1.98	.05	.36		2.39
55 The Procter & Gamble Company	30	.22	.05	.13		.39
56 Digital Equipment Corporation	30	1.27	.07	1.13		2.47

57	TRW Inc.	28	6.06	*	.15	6.22
58	Chesebrough-Pond's Inc.	28	2.12	*	.97	3.09
59	First Chicago Corporation	28	.89	.03	1.09	2.01
60	Florida Power & Light Company	27	2.07	.35	.82	3.25
61	Texas Utilities	27	1.61	.26	.28	2.15
62	Middle South Utilities, Inc.	27	2.70	.04	.83	3.57
63	Moore Corporation Limited	26	1.52	.03	.21	1.76
64	First International Bancshares, Inc.	26	2.54	.09	.97	3.60
65	Doubleday & Company, Inc.	26	8.16	15.36	6.81	30.33
66	The Chubb Corporation	25	.64	.76	2.76	4.16
67	Pennzoil Company	24	3.67	*	.35	4.02
68	United Telecommunications, Inc.	24	3.34	.02	.90	4.25
69	Armstrong Cork Company	24	4.22	.01	.05	4.27
70	Marcor Inc.	23	3.97	.01	.22	4.20
71	Textron Inc.	23	3.73	.02	.06	3.81
72	Carolina Power & Light Company	23	3.41	.04	1.17	4.62
73	First Bank System, Inc.	22	2.34	.04	.24	2.63

Issue	Market Value ($ Millions)	Percent of Outstanding Shares				
		Sole Voting (%)	Shared Voting (%)	No Voting (%)	Total Fiduciary Holdings (%)	
74 Matsushita Electric Industrial Co., Ltd.	22	1.15	.01	.22	1.37	
75 FMC Corporation	22	2.99	.01	1.16	4.16	
76 Southern California Edison Company	22	1.92	.02	.78	2.72	
77 Commonwealth Edison Company	21	.94	.04	.49	1.47	
78 Beatrice Foods Co.	20	.98	*	.29	1.27	
79 Schlumberger Limited	20	.07	.04	.31	.42	
80 Consumers Power Company	19	.63	.02	2.52	3.17	
81 Standard Oil Company of California	19	.19	.02	.11	.31	
82 Duke Power Company	18	1.79	.13	.86	2.77	
83 Marriott Corporation	18	2.42	.01	.67	3.10	
84 The Rank Organisation Limited	18	1.15	.01	.37	1.54	
85 Colonial Penn Group, Inc.	18	1.14	0	.79	1.93	
86 The Hobart Manufacturing Company	18	0	0	7.07	7.07	
87 Associated Dry Goods Corporation	17	4.60	*	.31	4.91	

88	Economics Laboratory, Inc.	17	3.12	.06	.24	3.42
89	The Louisiana Land and Exploration Company	16	.38	.04	.45	.88
90	General Mills, Inc.	16	.10	.01	1.12	1.22
91	Masco Corporation	16	2.33	.02	.72	3.08
92	The National Cash Register Company	16	.72	.05	1.33	2.11
93	Oklahoma Gas and Electric Company	15	3.32	*	.33	3.65
94	General Reinsurance Corporation	14	1.10	0	.20	1.30
95	The Lubrizol Corporation	14	1.36	.01	.54	1.90
96	Northern Indiana Public Service Company	14	3.39	.05	.46	3.90
97	Standard Oil Company (Ohio)	14	.19	0	.48	.68
98	International Flavors and Fragrances, Inc.	14	.46	.01	.52	.99
99	Southern Pacific Company	14	1.01	.02	.29	1.32
100	The Dow Chemical Company	14	.07	.02	.17	.26

Source for outstanding shares—Standard & Poor's Corporation Year-End 1973 Stock Guide.
*Less than .01%

DIRECTOR AFFILIATIONS

It has been suggested that bank trust departments are influenced by Board of Director relationships in making investment decisions for their customers. Although data was included in prior reports, we are simplifying access by providing a listing of the purchases and sales of common stock of companies where director relationships exist. Included are primary company affiliations of Citicorp/Citibank directors, plus the outside board affiliations of Citicorp/Citibank officers who also serve as directors.

COMMON STOCK PURCHASES AND SALES OF DIRECTOR AFFILIATED COMPANIES

January 1 — December 31, 1973	Bought ($000)	Rank in Top 500 Purchases	Sold ($000)	Rank in Top 500 Sales
Arlen Realty and Development Corporation	—	—	895	197
American Telephone and Telegraph Company	8,104	37	1,822	128
Beatrice Foods Co.	12,668	31	2,255	106
The Chubb Corporation	339	188	405	307
Continental Can Company, Inc.	6	453	200	429

Company				
Corning Glass Works	—	—	4,084	70
E. I. du Pont de Nemours & Company	36	313	4,658	67
Exxon Corporation	27,518	11	8,475	42
First National City Corporation	915	156	3,513	76
General Electric Company	11,958	32	12,249	24
International Business Machines Corporation	65,172	3	54,948	2
Kimberly-Clark Corporation	174	216	653	237
Monsanto Company	—	—	2,634	95
The National Cash Register Company	1,559	128	12,117	27
Owens-Illinois, Inc.	3	499	—	—
J. C. Penney Company, Inc.	26,853	12	11,539	28
Phelps Dodge Corporation	—	—	753	218
Phillips Petroleum Company	—	—	861	204
Sears, Roebuck and Co.	24,451	16	14,261	20
Standard Oil Company of California	106	238	2,929	86
Union Pacific Corporation	744	228	488	281
Xerox Corporation	77,026	1	31,802	8

MAJOR EQUITY PURCHASES AND SALES

The lists of major purchases and sales of equities during the previous year have been lengthened from 25 to 50. The lists are ranked by total cost of purchases and total proceeds from sales. In their entirety, IMG equity transactions in 1973 resulted in a modest net sale of common stock.

FIFTY LARGEST EQUITY PURCHASES BY MARKET VALUE
January 1 – December 31, 1973

	Issue	$ Millions		Issue	$ Millions
1	Xerox Corporation	$77	26	The Upjohn Company	14
2	Johnson & Johnson	74	27	Texas Instruments Incorporated	14
3	International Business Machines Corporation	65	28	Mobil Oil Corporation	14
4	Sony Corporation	64	29	Honeywell Inc.	13
5	Avon Products, Inc.	49	30	AMP Incorporated	13
6	Walt Disney Productions	47	31	Beatrice Foods Co.	13
7	Phillip Morris Incorporated	42	32	General Electric Company	12
8	Eli Lilly and Company	32	33	Baxter Laboratories, Inc.	11
			34	American Home Products Corporation	10
			35	The Lubrizol Corporation	10

#	Company	
9	S. S. Kresge Company	29
10	J. P. Morgan & Co. Incorporated	28
11	Exxon Corporation	28
12	J. C. Penney Company, Inc.	27
13	Merck & Co., Inc.	26
14	Matsushita Electric Industrial Co., Ltd.	26
15	Eastman Kodak Company	25
16	Sears, Roebuck and Co.	24
17	The Coca-Cola Company	23
18	Minnesota Mining and Manufacturing Company	22
19	First Chicago Corporation	22
20	American Express Company	21
21	Schering-Plough Corporation	19
22	Hewlett-Packard Company	17
23	Caterpillar Tractor Co.	16
24	Chesebrough-Pond's Inc.	16
25	The Bendix Corporation	15

#	Company	
36	Florida Power & Light Company	9
37	American Telephone and Telegraph Company	8
38	Duke Power Company	8
39	American Hospital Supply Corporation	8
40	The Black and Decker Manufacturing Company	8
41	Xerox Corporation	7
	(6% Convertible Debenture due 1995)	
42	Marriott Corporation	7
43	The Travelers Corporation	7
44	Digital Equipment Corporation	7
45	Atlantic Richfield Company	6
46	International Flavors & Fragrances, Inc.	6
47	Jonathan Logan, Inc.	6
48	Pabst Brewing Company	6
49	McCormick & Company, Incorporated	6
50	Automatic Data Processing, Inc.	6

FIFTY LARGEST EQUITY SALES BY MARKET VALUE

January 1 — December 31, 1973

	Issue	$ Millions		Issue	$ Millions
1	General Motors Corporation	$73	24	General Electric Company	12
2	International Business Machines Corporation	55	25	The Travelers Corporation	12
3	Ford Motor Company	53	26	General Mills, Inc.	12
4	Schering-Plough Corporation	52	27	The National Cash Register Company	12
5	International Telephone and Telegraph Corporation	50	28	J. C. Penney Company, Inc.	12
6	Merck & Co., Inc.	48	29	American Hospital Supply Corporation	11
7	The Louisiana Land and Exploration Company	40	30	Polaroid Corporation	11
8	Xerox Corporation	32	31	Marcor Inc.	11
9	Avon Products, Inc.	28	32	Transamerica Corporation	11
10	The Coca-Cola Company	27	33	Bristol-Myers Company	11
11	Eastman Kodak Company	25	34	The Southern Company	11
			35	Pennzoil Company	10
			36	Baxter Laboratories, Inc.	10

Rank	Company	Value
12	International Telephone and Telegraph Corporation ($2.25 Convertible Preferred)	19
13	Texas Instruments Incorporated	17
14	Minnesota Mining and Manufacturing Company	16
15	Union Oil Company of California ($2.50 Convertible Preferred)	16
16	American Home Products Corporation	16
17	Eli Lilly and Company	15
18	S. S. Kresge Company	15
19	Colonial Penn Group, Inc.	15
20	Sears, Roebuck and Co.	14
21	McDonald's Corporation	14
22	The Procter & Gamble Company	13
23	Squibb Corporation	13

Rank	Company	Value
37	Atlantic Richfield Company	9
38	International Flavors and Fragrances, Inc.	9
39	MGIC Investment Corporation	9
40	Zenith Radio Corporation	9
41	Union Oil Company of California	9
42	Exxon Corporation	8
43	Texaco Inc.	8
44	Motorola Inc.	8
45	Armstrong Cork Company	7
46	The Perkin-Elmer Corporation	7
47	Moore Corporation Limited	7
48	UAL, Incorporated	7
49	J. P. Morgan & Co. Incorporated	7
50	The Rank Organisation Limited	7

IV — INDEX

Account Officers, 33, 34
Acquisition loans, 29
Acquisitions 12, 28, 29
ACT program, of Citibank, 35, 36
Aircraft leasing, 31, 35
Aircraft manufacturers, 29, 30, 31
Airlines, 29, 30, 32
Alleged Conflicts, 38
Alleged nondisclosure of interest
    charges, 12
Atlantic Richfield, acquisition of
    Sinclair Oil by, 38

Balance of payments, 48
Bank-client relationships, 7, 17
Bankers, role of, in the regulatory
    process. See Bank regulation;
    also Regulatory agencies.
Bank examinations, 18, 46, 47
Bank examiners, federal and
    state, 18
Bank hiring practices. See
    Citibank, personnel practices;
    also Corwin, Professor
    R. David, study of.
Bank — holding company, 48
Banking for Government, 35
Bank regulation, 7, 18, 45
Banks, and the World Trade Center,
    39, 40
Base lending rate, 12
Beneficiary, 41, 42
Better Business Bureau, 25
Blacks, as employees of Citibank,
    15. See also Minority
        employees.
Boeing, 30
Bond transactions, 37

Branch lending activity, 33
Broker reciprocity, 4, 5, 11,
    37, 41
Brokers, 11, 37
Bureau of Labor Statistics, 14

"Campaign GM", 44
Capital gains, 4
Caplovitz, Professor David,
    study, "Debtors in
        Default", 23, 24
Cash balances, invested, 41
C.D.'s See Certificate of
    Deposit.
Certificate of Deposit, 47
Chapter-by-chapter response
    to Nader's "Citibank," 16
Checking accounts, 22, 35, 36, 37
Checking Plus, 12, 13
"Citibank," book by David
    Leinsdorf and Donald Etra, 1

Citibank (First National City
    Bank, FNCB):
    Account Officers, 33, 34
    ACT program, 35
    and Aircraft industries,
        airlines, 29, 30, 31
    and Aircraft leasing, 31, 35
    Approval of loans, 33
    and Bank examinations, 46, 47
    as a Bank holding company, 48
    Base lending rate to corporate
        customers, 12
    and Bank regulation, 7, 45
    Board of Directors, 9, 10, 31,
        32, 82, 83
    and Bond transactions, 37
    and Branch lending activity,
        28, 33

and Broker reciprocity, 4, 5,
11, 37, 41
Certificates of deposit,
(C.D.'s), 47
Checking accounts, 22, 35, 36, 37
Checking Plus, 12, 13
Collection practices, 25, 26
Commercial Department of,
6, 8, 41
Common trust funds, (CTF),
41, 42
Community development
activities, 32, 33
Comptroller's Department,
11
Confidential relationship
with customers, 7, 17
and Conflict of interest, 38
Consumer education, 33
Cooperation with the Fed,
25, 29, 40, 47, 48
Cooperation with the
Study Group, 17
Corporate Banking Group, 29
Corporate cash management
unit, 35
and Corporate customer
favoritism, 28
Corporate policy manual, 8, 11
Debt-to-income guidelines, 23
Delinquency record, loans, 24
Director affiliations, 9, 10,
31, 32, 41, 82, 83
Directors. See Citibank, Board
of Directors.
Disclosure of information
to study group, 17
Economic development
activity, 32

Employees:
Communication,
"Citiline", 21
Complaints, 21
Entry level, 14
Minority representa-
tion, 15, 19
Salaries, 13, 14, 19
Training programs, 20
Women, 15
as Employer, compared with
other banks, 18
and Equity kickers, 29
and Eurodollar market, 47, 48
Exchange of information
between Trust Department
and Commercial
Department, 6
FHA mortgage portfolio, 40
First Class Checking Account, 13
and "Front office" loans, 34
and General Motors Corpora-
tion, 44
and Hess-Amerada merger, 12
and Home mortgages, 40
Human resources pro-
grams, 33
Income tax returns and
credit files, 5
Information to state
and federal authorities, 7
Interest charges, 12
Investment Management Group,
(IMG), 2, 4, 6, 8, 9, 10, 11,
41, 42, 43, 61, 62, 63,
72, 73, 82, 83, 84
Investment Policy Committee,
8, 44
Job counseling, 33
JOBS program of, 19

Lending standards, 23, 33
Loan-to-deposit ratio, 28, 47
Loans to minority business, 32
Loans to public corporations,
    46
Master charge credit card, 13, 25
Memoranda to staff, 51, 52, 53,
    54, 55, 60
as a Money center bank, 48
and Municipal employee
    pension fund, 37
and National Advisory
    Committee, (NAC), 45, 46
New York City checking
    accounts, 35, 36, 37
Peat, Marwick, Mitchell & Co.,
    46, 47
and Penn Central Railroad, 5, 6,
    38, 39
Pension funds, 37, 43, 44
Personal checking accounts, 12
Personal loans, 11, 22, 23, 26
Personal Trust Department, 41, 42
Personnel practices, 13, 18, 21
Policy violations, 34
Portfolio turnovers, 41
Profit sharing accounts, 43, 44
Public disclosure, 6
Rebuttal and surrebuttal, 49
and Regulatory agencies, 7
Relations with customers, 7, 17
Reply to book by the
    Study Group, 3
Residential mortgage
    financing, 40
Retail customer services, 22
Salary grades, 13, 14, 19
and Savings institutions, 40, 45, 46
Self-examination and self-
    improvement programs, 49

and State and municipal
    securities, 35
and Transit fares, 39
Trust accounts, 4, 5, 10,
    12, 42
Trust Board, 9
Trust Department, 4, 8, 41,
    42
Use of trust funds, 8
Voting authority with stocks
    held, 72, 73
Working conditions at, 20, 21
and the World Trade Center,
    39, 40
Citibankers. See Citibank:
    Employees.

Citicorp (First National City
    Corporation, FNCC):
    Annual Report, 17
    Board of Directors, 10,
        31, 32, 82, 83
    Director affiliations, 10
    Stock of, 8
    Urban Affairs efforts, 32
Citicorp stock, voting of, 41
"Citiline", 21
Co-fiduciaries, 42
Colen, Donald J., 2, 53, 54, 55
Collection practices, 7, 22, 23,
    24, 25, 26, 27
Collins, Paul, 8, 11
Comment on appendices to Nader
    book, 49
Commercial banks, 45
Commercial Department, of
    Citibank, 6, 8, 41
Common trust funds (CTF),
    41, 42
Common trust funds of IMG.

See Investment Management
  Group.
Community development, 32, 33
Commuters, 38, 39
Competition for deposits, 40
Comptroller of the Currency,
  25, 45, 46, 47
Comptroller's Office, New York
  City, 37
Conflict of interest, 38
Consultant studies, of Citibank
  practices, 7, 18
Consumers, 33, 52, 53
Contradictions, by Study Group, 4
Cooperation, Citibank with Study
  Group, 6, 17, 51, 52, 53, 54,
  55, 60
Cooperation With The Fed, 47
Corporate Banking Group, of
  Citibank, 29
Corporate cash management unit,
  of Citibank, 35
Corporate customer favoritism, 11
Corwin, Professor R. David, 14,
  18, 19
Corwin, Professor R. David, study
  of New York City bank hiring
  practices by, 13, 14
Credit card. See Master Charge.
Credit extension, by Citibank, 22,
  23, 29
Credit files, of Citibank, 8
Credit, lines of, 47
Credit overloading, 23
Credit Policy Committee, of
  Citibank, 29
Credit unions, 46
Cresap, McCormick and Paget
  study, "Third Service Shopping
  Program", 22

Custodial accounts. See Investment
  Management Group
Customer complaints, 26
Customer service. See Citibank,
  retail customer services.

Debtor default, 25
"Debtors in Default". See
  Caplovitz, Professor David,
  study.
Debt-to-income guidelines, 23
Defaulting debtors, 23, 24
Degree of Investment Discretion,
  62, 63
Delinquent debtor, 26
Department of Labor, the, 13, 14
  18
Deposits, competition for, 40
Desch, Carl, 54
Director-affiliated companies, 9
Director affiliations, 9, 10, 31,
  32, 41, 82, 83
Directors of Citibank, 82, 83;
  See also Citibank, Board of
    Directors, and Citicorp
    Board of Directors
Disbursements to beneficiaries, 10
Disclosure, Citibank memoranda to
  officers, 51, 52, 53, 54, 55, 60
Disclosures by trust departments,
  6, 7. See also appendix tables
  and IMG, Annual Review.
Discretionary CTF's, 41, 42
DLMA. See Downtown Lower
  Manhattan Association.
Documents furnished to study
  group, 56, 57, 58, 59
Downtown Lower Manhattan
  Association, (DLMA), 39

Economic development, 32
Economic Development Center, 32
Employee complaints. See Citibank:
 employees.
Employee salaries. See Citibank:
 employee salaries
Employer's stock, pension funds,
 profit sharing plans, 43, 44
Equity holdings, of IMG, 6
Equity kickers, 29
Equity transactions, of IMG, 84
Equity security transactions, 11
Etra, Donald, 1
Eurodollar market transactions,
 47, 48
Examination of banks, 46, 47
Exceeding lending limits, 33
Excess of regulation, 45
Extension of credit, 28
Exter, John, 48
Exxon Corporation, 10

Favoritism, to corporate
 customers, by Citibank, 28
FDIC. See Federal Deposit
 Insurance Corporation.
Fed. See Federal Reserve Board.
Federal credit unions, 46
Federal Deposit Insurance
 Corporation, (FDIC), 45, 46
Federal Home Loan Bank System,
 46
Federal Housing Authority, (FHA),
 40
Federal Reserve Board, (Fed.),
 29, 40, 47, 48;
  Regulation Z, 25
  Restrictive monetary
   policy, 11, 12

Federal savings and loan associa-
 tions, 45, 46
Federal Savings and Loan Insurance
 Corporation, 46
Fiduciary medium. See Trusts,
 Common trust funds.
Figurative use of language, 1
Financial reports, of CTF, 42
Financing corporate concentration,
 28
First Class Checking Accounts, 13
First National City Bank, (FNCB).
 See Citibank.
First National City Corporation,
 (FNCC). See Citicorp.
Flying High With No Money Down,
 29, 30
FNCB (First National City Bank).
 See Citibank.
FNCC (First National City Cor-
 poration). See Citicorp.
Food stamp program, of New York
 City, 37
"Front office" loans, 34

General Electric Company, 31
General Motors Corporation, 44

Halsey Stuart & Co., 5, 37
Head security trader, 11
Hess Oil-Amerada Oil merger,
 12, 28, 29
Holding companies, 48. See also
 one-bank holding companies.
Home mortgages, 40
Human resources programs, 33
Human Rights, Division of.
 See New York State, Division
 of Human Rights.

IBM. See International Business
    Machines Corporation.
IMG. See Investment Management
    Group.
Improved customer services. See
    Citibank, retail customer
        services.
In Citibank We Trust, 41
Income tax returns:
    and Citibank credit files, 5
    of New York City, 5
Individual investment portfolios, 41
International Business Machines
    Corporation, (IBM), 10
International Telephone and
    Telegraph Corporation,
        (ITT), 10
Invested cash balances, 41
Investment Department, relations
    with Commercial Department.
        See Investment Manage-
        ment Group.
Investment discretion, 62, 63
Investment, in director-affiliated
    companies, 9
Investment Management Group,
    (IMG):
        Activities, 4, 10
        Annual Review, 2, 6, 8, 10, 61
        Bond holdings, 6
        Capital gains, 4
        Common trust funds, 9
        Custodial accounts, 10
        Customer portfolios and
            Citicorp stock, 8
        and Director-affiliated
            companies, 9, 41
        Equity holdings, 6
        Investment performance, 9, 41

            See also IMG Annual
                Review.
        and Investment Policy
            Committee, 8
        Pension funds, 9
        Personal trusts, 9
        and Regulatory review, 10
        Relations with other Citibank
            departments, 8
        Securities sales, 10
        Selection of brokers, 11
        Trust accounts, 4, 10
        and Uninvested cash balances,
            10
Investment performance of IMG.
    See Investment Management
        Group.
Investment Policy Board, 8
Investment Policy Committee, 8, 44
Investment Research Department,
    9
ITT. See International Telephone
    and Telegraph Corporation.

Job counseling, 33
Job Opportunity in the Business
    Sector (JOBS) program, 19

Kangaroo court, 7

Laeri, J. Howard, 9, 48, 54, 55
Leinsdorf, David, 1, 54, 55, 56
Lending standards, of Citibank,
    23, 24, 25, 33
Lindsay, Mayor John V., 39
Lines of credit, 47
Loans for housing and community
    facilities, 33

Loans to low-income individuals,
23, 25
Loan-to-deposit ratio, 28, 47
Lockheed, 30, 31
Long Island Railroad, 38

Major equity purchases and sales
by IMG, 84-89
Martin Marietta, acquisition of
Harvey Aluminum by, 28, 29
Master Charge credit cards, 13, 25
McDonnell-Douglas, 30
Methodology:
of Ralph Nader, 1
of Study Group, 12
Metropolitan Transportation
Authority, (MTA), 38, 39
Minority business loans, 32
Minority employees, of Citibank,
15, 19
Money center bank, 48
Monsanto Company, 10
Moore, George S., 45, 46
MTA. See Metropolitan Transpor-
tation Authority.
Municipal employee pension fund,
37

Nader, Ralph, 1, 52, 53, 54, 55
Nader Study Group. See Study
Group.
NAC. See National Advisory
Committee.
National Advisory Committee
(NAC), 45, 46
National Advisory Panel of Project
on Computer Data Banks, 52
National banks, influence of, on
the Comptroller's Office.
See Comptroller.

National Cash Register Company,
(NCR), 10
National Organization of Women,
(NOW), 15
NCR. See National Cash Register
Company.
New Haven Railroad, commuter
operations, 38, 39
New York City:
Bonds, 39
Checking accounts, 35, 36, 37
Comptroller's Office, 37
Economic and social problems,
37
Food stamp program, 37
Income tax returns, 5
Officials, 5
Pension fund transactions, 5, 49
Taxing powers, 39
Transit fares, 39
Welfare check distribution, 37
New York State:
Division of Human Rights, 20
Public Officers law, 38
Nixon Administration, the, 31
Nondisclosure of interest charges
by Citibank, 12
NOW. See National Organization
of Women.

One-Bank Holding Companies, 48
Opinion Research Corporation,
(ORC), study of employees,
20, 21

Palmer, Edward L., 8
Peat, Marwick, Mitchell & Co.,
46, 47
Penn Central Railroad, 5, 6, 37, 38
Pension fund holdings in

employer's stock, 43
Pension funds, 49. See also
    Citibank: Pension funds;
    New York City: Pension
    funds; and IMG.
Personal checking accounts, 12
Personal loans, 7, 11, 22, 23, 26, 52
Personal Trust Department, of
    Citibank, 41, 42
Personal trusts of IMG. See
    Investment Management Group
Personnel policies, of Citibank,
    13, 21
Personnel studies, 13
Policy violations, 34
Portfolio turnovers, 41
Predetermined conclusions, of
    Study Group, 1, 4
Presumption of guilt technique, 4
    See also Study Group, approach,
    and New York City, income
    tax returns.
Prime rate, 30
Privileged tax status, 40
Process servers, 27
"Profile of a City", 37
Profit sharing plans, employer's
    stock, 43, 44
Public disclosure by Citibank.
    See Citibank.
Public Officers Law, section 73, 38
Pyne, Eben W., 38, 39

Rate of return, on securities, 35
Rebuttal, 49
Reciprocity, brokers. See Broker
    reciprocity.
Regulation of banks. See Bank
    regulations and Regulatory
    agencies.

Regulation of trust departments, 10
Regulation Z. See Federal Reserve
    Board, Regulation.
Regulatory agencies, 18, 45
Relationship between Trust Dept.
    and Commercial Dept., 41
Research Methodology, 21
    See also Methodology.
Reserve requirements, 47, 48
Residential mortgage financing,
    40
Retail Banking for Individuals,
    22
Rockefeller, Governor Nelson A.,
    38
Rolls Royce, 30

Salary grades. See Citibank,
    salary grades.
Savings accounts, 40
Savings institutions, 40
Savings and loan associations,
    45, 46
Sawyer, David A., 15
Scott, George C., 29
Sears, Roebuck & Co., 10
Securities.
    Government, 35
    Penn Central, 5-6
    Pension funds, profit sharing
        accounts, 43, 44
    State and municipal, 35
Separation of Trust and Commercial
    Departments, 6, 8
Shadow warrants, 29
Sinclair Oil, acquisition by Atlantic
    Richfield, 28
Smith, Lamson B., 53
Spencer, William I., 8, 52
Student loans, 52

Study group, the, 1, 6
   Cooperation with, by Citibank
      6, 51, 52, 53, 54, 55, 60
   First report, 1971, 6
   Research methodology, 12
Surrebuttal, 49

Temporary cash balances, 10
"The Factory"; 20
The World Trade Center, 39, 40
"Third Service Shopping Program",
   study by Cresap, McCormick and
      Paget, 22
Thrift savings plans, employer's
   stock, 43, 44
Training programs at Citibank. See
   Citibank: employees.
Trust accounts, 4, 10, 12. See also
   IMG, trust accounts.
Trust funds, 5, 8
Trust Department and Commercial
   Banking relations, 4, 41
Truth-in-Lending Act, 25

Underwriting of state and
   municipal securities by banks.
      See Securities.
Uninvested cash balances, 4, 10
United Aircraft Corporation, 31
United Nations, inquiry on multina-
   tional corporations, 1
Unsecured loans, 26
Urban Affairs efforts, 32
U.S. Department of Labor. See
   Department of Labor.

Voting authority, 72, 73
Voting control, over stock in
   Trust Department, 8

Wadsworth, Ms. Beverly, 20
Wages at Citibank. See Citibank:
   employee salaries.
Wall, alleged, between commercial
   and trust departments, 8
Warrants, 29
Welfare check distribution, 37
Who Doesn't Get Credit, 32
Who Gets Credit, 28
Wilcox, Thomas R., 9
Women, as employees of Citibank,
   15
Wriston, Walter B., 2, 8, 31, 51,
   52, 53, 54, 55, 60

Xerox Corporation, 10

Zero balance system, 35